Gambling Trends

ISSUES

Volume 129

Series Editor

Lisa Firth

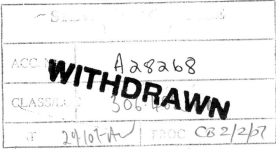
 *Independence*

Educational Publishers
Cambridge

First published by Independence
PO Box 295
Cambridge CB1 3XP
England

British Library Cataloguing in Publication Data
Gambling Trends – (Issues Series)
I. Firth, Lisa II. Series
363.4'2

ISBN 978 1 86168 375 5

Printed in Great Britain
MWL Print Group Ltd

Cover
The illustration on the front cover is by
Simon Kneebone.

CONTENTS

Chapter One: Gambling in the UK

Gambling	1
Forms of gambling	2
The Gambling Commission	4
The science of gambling	6
Governing gambling	8
Key facts about the National Lottery	9
Lottery timeline	10
Under 16s and the National Lottery	11
UK's first supercasino	14
Q&A: Supercasino	15
Risks of the 'supercasino'	16
Interactive or remote gambling	17
Are there any benefits to gambling?	18

Chapter Two: Cybergambling

Boom in online gambling	19
Online gambling in Europe	20
Online gambling drives addiction rates	21
Internet betting	21
Gambling at work	22
£1m online loser jailed	24

Online poker hooks teenagers	25
Mobile gambling boom time ahead	26

Chapter Three: Problem Gambling

The problem with gambling	27
Information on gambling	28
Gambling 'as addictive as crack cocaine'	30
Doctors fear boom in gambling addiction	31
One in 10 Scottish children is gambling addict	32
Story of a teenage problem gambler	33
More women seeking help over gambling addiction	34
Signs and interventions for a gambling dependency	35
Gambling debt	36
Gamblers Anonymous and GamAnon	37
Drug may curb pathological gambling	39

Key Facts	40
Glossary	41
Index	42
Additional Resources	43
Acknowledgements	44

Introduction

Gambling Trends is the one hundred and twenty-ninth volume in the **Issues** series. The aim of this series is to offer up-to-date information about important issues in our world.

Gambling Trends looks at current developments concerning gambling in the UK, the growing issue of gambling via the Internet and mobile telephones, and problem gambling.

The information comes from a wide variety of sources and includes:
Government reports and statistics
Newspaper reports and features
Magazine articles and surveys
Website material
Literature from lobby groups
and charitable organisations.

It is hoped that, as you read about the many aspects of the issues explored in this book, you will critically evaluate the information presented. It is important that you decide whether you are being presented with facts or opinions. Does the writer give a biased or an unbiased report? If an opinion is being expressed, do you agree with the writer?

Gambling Trends offers a useful starting-point for those who need convenient access to information about the many issues involved. However, it is only a starting-point. Following each article is a URL to the relevant organisation's website, which you may wish to visit for further information.

* * * * *

Gambling

Basic facts and figures

What is gambling?

There is no clear-cut definition of gambling, but it does have a number of common elements:

⇨ Two or more people agree to take part in the activity (usually the operator and the person who wishes to gamble);

⇨ The stake (usually money) is transferred from the loser to the winner;

⇨ The outcome is uncertain;

⇨ The result is determined (partly) by chance;

⇨ Participation is active – the individual has to be involved in the transaction.

A historical look at gambling

⇨ **2000 BC** Egyptians used knucklebones painted as four-sided dice.

⇨ **1500 BC** in China, spinning discs were used as a game of roulette.

⇨ **AD 210** the first recorded horse race took place (in England).

⇨ **1588** the first lottery was approved in Britain (as Queen Elizabeth I needed to raise funds to repair the Cinque Ports).

⇨ **1895** Charles Fey, a mechanic from San Francisco produced the first slot machine. It was a commercial success in America and machines came to the UK a few years later.

⇨ **1906** gambling in public was prohibited by the Street Betting Act.

⇨ **1926** the first greyhound race in Britain was held in Manchester.

⇨ **1926** Winston Churchill imposed a betting tax (this was abolished three years later – but reimposed in 1967).

⇨ **1960** the Betting and Gaming Act legalised betting shops in Britain. Before the law was passed there was widespread crime and racketeering controlling (illegal) gambling which was very popular in this country.

⇨ **1964** Gamblers Anonymous was founded in the UK (having originated in America).

⇨ The National Lottery was launched in November 1994, and scratchcards were introduced in March 1995.

⇨ In 1996 betting shops were allowed to have (a maximum of two) fruit machines for the first time.

Why is gambling so popular?

We like gambling because:

⇨ It is fun and entertaining.

⇨ It is easily accessible (in shops, arcades, on the high street etc.)

⇨ It offers the chance to win money/prizes.

⇨ It is accepted as part of our culture.

⇨ It offers an escape, a fantasy, a chance to take risks.

⇨ It can provide a challenge or element of skill.

⇨ It can provide a feeling of being in control.

⇨ It can give you a natural buzz/adrenalin rush.

⇨ It can be a social activity.

⇨ It is glamorised in the media, and in adverts.

Who gambles?

⇨ There are around 300,000 adult problem gamblers in Britain.

⇨ 76% of men and 68% of women gambled in the past year.

⇨ 75% of teenagers gamble.

⇨ Gambling activities are available for all age groups.

⇨ Popular gambling activities in our society are: National Lottery and scratchcards, football pools, fruit/slot machines, bingo, betting on horse/dog racing, gambling in casinos, betting on sports events, private card games, raffles. Increasingly, opportunities to gamble are becoming available through new technology, e.g. Internet, WAP phones, Interactive Television.

Young people and gambling

A survey of 12 to 15-year-olds conducted by Sue Fisher (published 1998) found:

⇨ 75% had played fruit/slot machines;

⇨ 47% had played National Lottery scratchcards;

⇨ 40% had played the National Lottery draw;

⇨ 7% had been illegally sold tickets;

⇨ 5% showed signs of gambling addiction.

Gambling facts*

⇨ Gambling turnover is £42 billion per year – which equals £115 million a day!

⇨ £1.5 billion goes to the government in taxes!

⇨ An estimated £9 billion is staked per year on fruit/slot machines.

⇨ Around £6 billion is gambled on horse racing.

⇨ £30 billion has been gambled on the National Lottery since its launch.

* Figures last collated in 1999 and have widely believed to have grown since.

Is gambling harmful?

Like most things, gambling is fine in moderation, but if done to excess it can become addictive. Individuals can become dependent on gambling and a lot of damage can be caused to the individual and his or her family. A small but significant number of men, women and young gamblers become addicted.

Addiction to gambling can be as destructive as a drug or alcohol dependency. The gambling addict destroys relationships with family and friends, and may jeopardise his or her education, job or career. In some cases they may resort to crime to fund their 'habit'. This can mean losing possessions, job, home or family, and a prison sentence or community sentence. Gambling addicts are also at high risk of attempting suicide when their situation goes out of control, and they may suffer depression, low self-esteem, and physical side effects from stress.

Unfortunately, a gambling problem is hard to identify, and the gambler will have become used to lying to cover the telltale signs. Often the gambling addiction is discovered because other problems have occurred – such as serious debt, eviction orders, court notices, relationship breakdown, or a criminal conviction. It is estimated that gambling addiction in adults can affect around 13 other people, from the partner, children, siblings and parents through to friends, colleagues and employers.

Problem areas

In 2001, problem areas identified by those calling our Helpline for the first time were as follows:

⇨ 53.5% Fruit machines
⇨ 29.5% Horses
⇨ 6.5% Casino

⇨ 2.1% Bingo
⇨ 0.5% Scratchcards
⇨ 0.1% Private card games.

A healthy approach to gambling

In order to keep gambling under control, and prevent problems from occurring, consider the following points:

⇨ You are buying entertainment – not investing your money.

⇨ Before gambling, set strict limits on how much time and money you are going to spend.

⇨ Quit when you are ahead.

⇨ Only gamble with money you can afford to lose.

⇨ Do not chase your losses.

⇨ Keep up other hobbies and interests to ensure that gambling does not take over.

⇨ Gambling in moderation is okay and healthy.

GamCare helpline: 0845 6000 133

⇨ The above information is reprinted with kind permission from GamCare, the National Association for Gambling Care. Visit www.gamcare.org.uk for more information.

© GamCare

Forms of gambling

Information from GamCare

A sporting bet

One of the most popular forms of gambling is betting. This generally involves placing a bet on a sporting event at a bookmaker's – horse racing is the most popular event. The amount an individual can win depends on the amount staked and the odds (probability) of that horse winning. Other events that are popular with gamblers include dog racing and football.

Betting machines

Another popular gambling activity is playing on fruit machines, also known as slot machines or one-armed bandits. There are also similar machines in Australia called 'pokies' (video poker machines).

Casino games

Casinos have the greatest variety of games available in one venue. As well as playing on high-jackpot slot machines, gamblers can play various card games such as poker and blackjack, try their hand at craps, or take a chance at the roulette table. Casinos differ from other gambling venues because gambling chips are used instead of money. These are small, coloured discs, each with a different monetary value. Gamblers purchase the chips in a casino in order to gamble on the tables.

Bingo

A numbers game where the winner has to be the first one to match random numbers printed on a card to those being called out.

Lottery

A chance numbers game where the customer has to select the winning numbers drawn out. The jackpot is a percentage of the money collected from everyone playing. Lotteries are often used to collect money for charity.

Spread betting

A high-risk form of gambling popular with people wishing to bet on the stock exchange and sporting events. Winnings can be large but gamblers have less control over how much they may lose.

Taken from Need to Know Gambling (Smeaton & Bellringer 2003)

⇨ The above information is reprinted with kind permission from GamCare. Visit www.gamcare.org.uk for more information.

© GamCare

Statistics taken from *Gambling or Gaming: Entertainment or Exploitation?*

Percentage of UK adults gambling during the previous 12 months

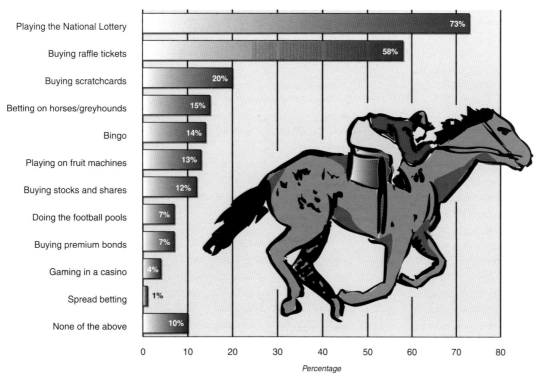

Playing the National Lottery	73%
Buying raffle tickets	58%
Buying scratchcards	20%
Betting on horses/greyhounds	15%
Bingo	14%
Playing on fruit machines	13%
Buying stocks and shares	12%
Doing the football pools	7%
Buying premium bonds	7%
Gaming in a casino	4%
Spread betting	1%
None of the above	10%

Percentage

Source: Gaming review report; note: percentages do not add up to 100% because participants could give more than one answer

Gaming machines by location

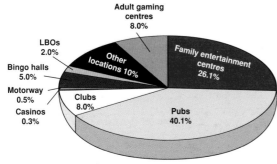

Adult gaming centres 8.0%
LBOs 2.0%
Other locations 10%
Bingo halls 5.0%
Motorway 0.5%
Casinos 0.3%
Clubs 8.0%
Family entertainment centres 26.1%
Pubs 40.1%

Source: Gaming Board 04/05

Total revenues from mobile gambling, 2009 (US$19,320.5m)

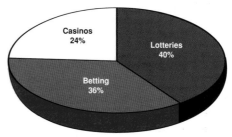

Casinos 24%
Lotteries 40%
Betting 36%

Source: Juniper Research, White Paper – Gambling on mobile

Lotto participation per social group

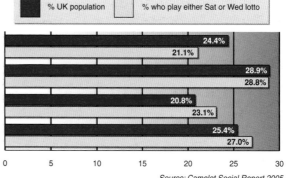

█ % UK population	☐ % who play either Sat or Wed lotto

	% UK population	% who play either Sat or Wed lotto
AB (occupation, higher/intermediate managerial, administrative or professional)	24.4%	21.1%
C1 (occupation: supervisory or clerical, junior managerial, administrative or professional)	28.9%	28.8%
C2 (occupation: skilled manual workers)	20.8%	23.1%
DE (occupation: semi and unskilled manual workers, state pensioners or widows [no other earner], casual or lowest grade workers)	25.4%	27.0%

Source: Camelot Social Report 2005

The Gambling Commission

Frequently asked questions

What is the size of the gambling industry in the UK?

The estimated annual turnover of gambling activities in the UK is about £53 billion, according to 2005 figures from the National Audit Office.

What proportion of British people gamble?

The latest British gambling Prevalence Study, published in 2000, suggested that almost three-quarters (72%) of the population took part in some sort of gambling activity within the past year. Excluding the National Lottery 46% of people participated in gambling activities.

The Gambling Commission is commissioning a new Prevalence Study, which will be published in 2007.

What are the most popular gambling activities?

According to the last Prevalence Study the most popular gambling activity in Britain is lotteries, especially the National Lottery, with some two-thirds of the population having bought a lottery ticket in the past year. The second most popular gambling activity is the purchase of scratchcards, with one in five (22%) people purchasing scratchcards in the past year. This is followed by fruit machines (14%) and betting on horseracing (13%).

What is the difference between the Gaming Board for Great Britain and the Gambling Commission?

The Gaming Board for Great Britain was established under the 1968 Gaming Act. It regulated casinos, bingo, gaming machines and certain lotteries.

The Gambling Commission has been established by the Gambling Act 2005. It replaced and took over the functions of the Gaming Board on 1 October 2005. In addition, it will have responsibility from 2007 for the regulation of betting and remote gambling, as well as helping to protect children and vulnerable people. The Commission is also responsible for advising local and central government on issues related to gambling.

What difference will this make to the way in which the industry is regulated?

The Commission has been set up to regulate all commercial gambling in Great Britain (other than spread betting and the National Lottery). It has a wider role than the Gaming Board and, from 2007, will have greater powers to ensure that gambling is conducted in a manner that meets the statutory objectives of keeping out crime, being fair and open and protecting children and the vulnerable.

How is the Commission funded?

The Commission is funded by grant-in-aid from the Department for Culture, Media and Sport. The Commission is required to cover its expenditure on operations through the fees charged for certification and licensing. This fee income is surrendered to DCMS.

When the 2005 Act licensing regime comes fully into effect in 2007 the current DCMS grant-in-aid for operational costs will be replaced by direct fee income which the Commission will retain. Some DCMS grant in aid will continue for some additional areas of Commission work relating to research and enforcement.

The most popular gambling activity in Britain is lotteries, especially the National Lottery, with some two-thirds of the population having bought a lottery ticket in the past year

---

How does the Gambling Commission maintain impartiality?

The Gambling Commission is an independent statutory regulator. It is responsible for advising government on issues related to gambling either at the specific request of Ministers or in the light of new developments. It is accountable to Parliament via the Secretary of State for its actions and has undertaken to make its processes as clear and transparent as practicable.

How will the Commission protect children and vulnerable people?

When the Gambling Act 2005's provisions come fully into force in 2007 the Commission's new licensing conditions and codes of practice will require the industry to take particular measures to protect children and the vulnerable. These codes will be issued for consultation early in 2006.

The Commission will work closely with the Responsibility in Gambling Trust (RIGT). The RIGT currently has the role of commissioning services and activities to aim to raise awareness about problem gambling and community treatment, prevention and education and research into problem gambling (see www.rigt.org.uk).

Who runs the Commission?

The Commission is directed by nine Commissioners, chaired by Peter Dean and including Chief Executive Jenny Williams. Biographical details can be found in the About Us section of the Gambling Commission website.

Who is the organisation accountable to?

The Commission – like its predecessor the Gaming Board – is accountable to the Secretary of State and Parliament for its performance.

It will publish performance indicators and will produce an Annual Report on its activities.

72% of the population took part in some sort of gambling activity within the past year. Excluding the National Lottery 46% of people participated in gambling activities

---

Why is the Commission relocating to Birmingham?

The decision to relocate to Birmingham follows the Government's policy that new public bodies should be located outside London and the South East. The Commission considered a shortlist of possible locations which were evaluated against the Commission's business requirements and the Government's wider economic impact criteria. Birmingham was chosen.

When does the Act come into force?

The Gambling Act 2005 received Royal Assent in April 2005.

The Department for Culture, Media and Sport (DCMS) is responsible for developing regulations under the Act and bringing sections of the Act into force as necessary. These are expected to come fully into force in 2007.

What precisely is the Commission's relationship with the DCMS?

The Gambling Commission is independent of Government.

It is an executive non-Departmental Public Body, sponsored by the Department for Culture, Media and Sport and accountable to Parliament via the Secretary of State.

The Commission receives grant in aid from the Department. The Commission's Funding Agreement with DCMS is available on the Gambling Commission website.

What will the Commission regulate?

The Gambling Commission has taken over the role of the Gaming Board for Great Britain in regulating casinos, bingo, gaming machines and certain lotteries. From 2007, it will also regulate betting and remote gambling.

The Commission does not regulate spread betting (which is regulated by the Financial Services Authority) or the National Lottery (which is regulated by the National Lottery Commission).

What powers will the Commission have?

When the 2005 Act is fully in force in 2007, the Commission will have the following powers:

⇨ It may impose conditions on the licences it grants, and it will issue codes of practice.

⇨ It will be able to review licences.

⇨ Sanctions available to it will include formal warnings, the amendment of licence conditions, imposition of financial penalties of any amount, and licence revocation.

⇨ Its staff will have powers of entry, search and seizure.

⇨ It will have enforcement powers to tackle illegal gambling and cheating and will be able to initiate criminal proceedings.

What role will the Gambling Commission have in ensuring problem gamblers receive treatment for their addiction?

Treatment for problem gamblers is currently funded by the industry through the Responsibility in Gambling Trust (through, for example, organisations such as GamCare or Gordon House, which help and treat addicted gamblers).

The Commission will work with operators to ensure that information about where to get help or treatment is made available in gambling venues and on remote gambling platforms. This will help to ensure that an individual who is experiencing problems with their gambling is aware of where to get help.

What licensing conditions will the Commission impose?

The pre-2005 Act licensing regime will continue to apply until 2007.

The Commission will be consulting on proposed licence conditions and code of practice from early 2006. Anyone who has an interest is encouraged to register online to receive information and updates on the consultation process.

⇨ Information from the Gambling Commission. Visit www.gamblingcommission.gov.uk for more information.

© Gambling Commission

The science of gambling

David Brill looks at the psychological, biological and social factors that drive people to gamble

Gutshot is London's first dedicated poker club and now the biggest of its kind in Europe. In a little over two years it has acquired some 15,000 members, expanding from a few tables in a dingy basement to take over the spacious bar complex next door. The success of Gutshot is symptomatic of a wider trend – and it's not just poker that is on the rise: gambling is everywhere and spreading fast. Britain is on the verge of opening its first 'supercasino', in addition to over 130 existing casinos. Fruit machines, blackjack, roulette – even bingo is becoming more popular.

Tax calculations suggest that 78% of the British population gambled at some point during 2005

So why do people gamble? What makes it so enjoyable? Why do some people become addicted while others simply enjoy a flutter on the horses every now and then? And could drug therapy be the answer to problem gambling?

John Ioannou is the card-room manager at Gutshot. With a firsthand experience of gambling, Ioannou understands the emotion that accompanies success at the poker table. 'The elation of winning, obviously, is great. It's a buzz you can't tell anybody about unless they've actually done it themselves. You're on cloud cuckoo land for a little while.'

But losing also involves its fair share of emotion. Ioannou remembers feeling sick after losing up to £1,000 ($1,898) in one session. Gambling involves abandoning

self-control and he says that even if a gambler limits the amount of money he will gamble, once at the poker club, his mindset often changes. 'You go to the card-room, you do your 200 quid ($380), pull up another 200 quid ($380), then another 200 quid ($380). Now your mind's not straight, it's not as clear as when you left home', he says.

Gambling psychology

So what exactly is going on in a gambler's mind? Professor Peter Collins, director of the Centre for the Study of Gambling at Salford University, does research related to ethics and gambling, problem gambling and Internet gambling. 'Why people gamble is a good and puzzling question,' he says. 'On the face of it, it looks very strange that people should stand in front of machines and pour money into

them, knowing that they're going to lose.'

But gamblers don't seem to be thinking of the financial loss when they're in front of a slot machine – what draws people to gambling seems to be the thrill of playing and the hope of a big win. Collins says that if you asked a gambler how much he hoped to win and then offered him that money provided he didn't gamble, the gambler would refuse. Similarly, if you told him he could gamble but there would be no money involved, it would take the fun out of it and he wouldn't be interested.

Different forms of gambling each have their own appeal and someone who plays casino games gets a different kind of thrill from someone who buys lottery tickets. Collins says that the buzz experienced from playing a casino game is similar to the thrill of riding a roller coaster. In contrast, buying a lottery ticket fuels a person's financial fantasy life. 'I sometimes describe it as soft financial pornography,' he says. 'It spices up the fantasy of being suddenly and fantastically rich.'

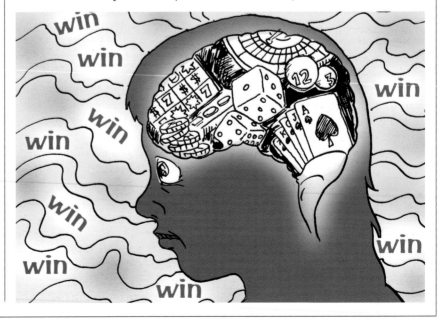

Neurobiology and problem gambling

Tax calculations suggest that 78% of the British population gambled at some point during 2005. Yet the rates of problem gambling in this country are relatively low, standing at less than 1% of the population. With such a discrepancy, the issue of pathological gambling has begun to move from the realm of sociology to neuroscience in an attempt to explain why some people find gambling so much more addictive than others.

One thing is for sure – the emotional highs and lows will always be a key part of the attraction of gambling

---

A study has found that there is less activity in the ventromedial prefrontal cortex area of the brain of pathological gamblers.

Research in this field is being led by American researchers and at the Problem Gambling Clinic at the Yale University School of Medicine, scientists are studying the neurobiology of pathological gambling. Some of the work done by Dr Marc Potenza, an associate professor at the clinic, involves looking at the differences in brain activation between pathological gamblers and people who don't gamble. One study has already found that the ventromedial prefrontal cortex, an area of the brain involved in decision-making and impulse control, is less active in pathological gamblers. 'Less activation of this brain region is often found in individuals with impulsive aggression, and it's also been implicated in mood disorders,' says Potenza.

Linking the condition to a specific region of the brain has raised the possibility of targeted drug therapies. The clinic has been involved in treatment trials, including the largest study published to date looking at the use of a drug called Nalmefene to treat pathological gambling.

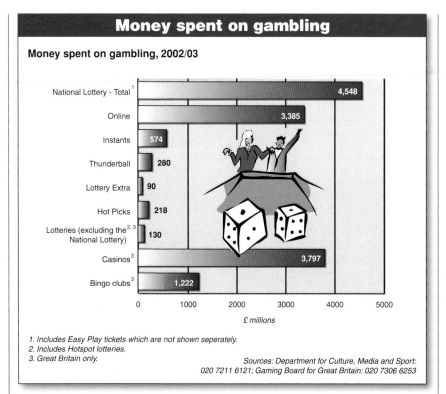

Money spent on gambling

Money spent on gambling, 2002/03

Category	£ millions
National Lottery - Total [1]	4,548
Online	3,385
Instants	574
Thunderball	280
Lottery Extra	90
Hot Picks	218
Lotteries (excluding the National Lottery) [2,3]	130
Casinos [3]	3,797
Bingo clubs [3]	1,222

1. Includes Easy Play tickets which are not shown seperately.
2. Includes Hotspot lotteries.
3. Great Britain only.

Sources: Department for Culture, Media and Sport: 020 7211 6121; Gaming Board for Great Britain: 020 7306 6253

Nalmefene is thought to act on brain circuits containing the chemical dopamine, which form a key component of the brain's natural reward system. Reducing activity in these brain cells should reduce the natural highs felt when gambling. 'The drug was found to be superior to a placebo in terms of reducing gambling-related thoughts and behaviours,' says Potenza.

Social factors at play?

Some, however, are less keen to label pathological gambling as a medical disorder. Dr Scott Vrecko, a sociologist at the London School of Economics (LSE), stresses the importance of other factors: 'If there are no casinos or opportunities to gamble in a city, that city is not going to have very many gambling problems. If the proportion of individuals involved in gambling rises, the number of people with gambling problems is going to rise too.'

Vrecko is against the 'medicalisation' of different aspects of life and doesn't think that complex social problems like gambling have a strictly biological basis. 'I think that we should be wary of moving too far towards primarily medical explanations,' he explains.

The appeal of gambling is probably a complex interaction between biological, social and psychological factors. In the wake of the current gambling boom, particularly on the Internet, only time will tell whether problem gambling becomes more prevalent, and whether drug treatments will prove a successful solution.

But one thing is for sure – the emotional highs and lows will always be a key part of the attraction of gambling. 'I remember the first tournament I won,' recalls John. 'I thought I was the best poker player in the world. When we're winning we think we're great, but when we're losing we just can't understand why.'

For more information

University of Salford – Centre for the Study of Gambling
http://www.gamblingstudies.salford.ac.uk/
Rochester Institute of Technology – Factors Contributing to the Development of Pathological Gambling
http://www.personalityresearch.org/papers/sinha.html

⇨ The above information is reprinted with kind permission from FirstScience.com. Visit www.firstscience.com for more information.

© FirstScience.com

Governing gambling

Gambling Commission publishes proposed new rules to govern gambling in Britain

The Gambling Commission has today published a draft of the new rules which will govern British gambling in future.

The changes are being introduced under the Gambling Act 2005. They are designed to secure the Act's three objectives of keeping crime out of gambling, making sure gambling is fair and open and protecting children and vulnerable people from harm. They will apply to casinos, bingo clubs, lotteries and gaming machines, as well as betting and online gambling which are being brought under the Gambling Commission's jurisdiction for the first time.

The Commission's Licence Conditions and Codes of Practice set out a raft of provisions, including new rules designed to combat problem gambling.

Amongst the key points are:

⇨ All gambling operators must have published policies and procedures for promoting socially responsible gambling. These must include how they will contribute to research, to education about the risks of gambling, and to the treatment of problem gamblers.

⇨ Information about responsible gambling and help available to problem gamblers must be prominently displayed wherever gambling takes place, as well as in discreet areas such as toilets. Online operators must make this information accessible on their home and login pages.

⇨ Operators must exclude people in cases where there are clear signs of problem gambling, and customers who feel they have a problem must also be able to exclude themselves.

⇨ Casino and bingo operators must introduce measures to control continuous and repetitive play, such as designing sites and implementing procedures to encourage breaks in play and making customers aware of the time they have spent gambling.

Alcohol must not be used as an inducement to encourage people to gamble. Strict technical standards will be imposed to control the speed of gaming machines. Online operators must make sure that customers are aware of how much time and money they have spent on their sites.

⇨ Operators must train their staff about problem gambling and about dealing with customers who may be affected.

'What can be a harmless pastime for one person can be a life-destroying addiction for another'

⇨ Operators must follow strict procedures to prevent underage gambling, including age checks on anyone who appears to be under 21. Specific rules will apply to casinos, which will be required to employ trained supervisors to keep anyone underage away from gambling. Online operators must carry out random credit card checks, and filtering software must be made available to allow adults to block access by children and young people.

⇨ Key staff such as managing and finance directors must be licensed by the Commission, as must casino employees such as dealers and cashiers. The application process for those licences is an important step in keeping crime out of gambling.

⇨ The rules of games, odds, house edge and average return to the player must all be clearly displayed, and operators must have well-publicised complaints procedures which include an external, independent element.

Gambling Commission Chairman Peter Dean said: 'Our new rules are all designed to keep crime out of gambling, to make sure it is fair and open, and to protect children and vulnerable people. Combating problem gambling is particularly important to us: this is the first time the Commission has had the power to do something about it, and we intend to use that power to maximum effect. We've drawn from international experience to make sure that standards of social responsibility amongst gambling operators will be the highest in the world.

'We will monitor all British gambling operators to make sure they comply with our rules. We have the power to fine or revoke the licences of those who fail to do so, and to prosecute illegal gambling. We won't hesitate to use these powers if need be.'

Secretary of State for Culture, Media and Sport Tessa Jowell said: 'Gambling is not an industry like any other. What can be a harmless pastime for one person can be a life-destroying addiction for another. That's why these new rules to prevent problem gambling are so important. Be it a betting shop, a casino or a gambling website, gambling operators across the country will soon have to comply with these tough requirements. Without the Gambling Act this would not have been possible.'

The Gambling Commission's Licence Conditions and Codes of Practice are being published for consultation, with responses due by 2 June 2006. The new conditions and codes will apply from September 2007, when the Gambling Act 2005 comes fully into force.

As well as the new rules, the Commission has published a policy paper on problem gambling, which sets out the background to its approach to this issue.
10 March 2006

⇨ Information from the Gambling Commission. Visit www.gamblingcommission.gov.uk for more information.

© Gambling Commission

Key facts about the National Lottery

Information from Camelot

Good causes

⇨ National Lottery players have helped to raise more than £19 billion for Good Causes to date.

⇨ More than 240,000 individual awards have been made across the UK in the biggest programme of civic regeneration since the 19th century – that is an average of 79 lottery grants for every single postcode district.

⇨ At over 40% of total sales (28% to the Good Causes and 12% in lottery duty), Camelot returns a higher proportion of lottery revenue to society than any other major lottery operator in the world.

⇨ Each week over £25 million is generated for the Good Causes.

Winners and prizes

⇨ Over £28.1 billion has been paid out in prizes since launch.

⇨ On average, more than 4 million people win prizes every week on the National Lottery's draw-based games and scratchcards.

⇨ Over 1,900 millionaires or multi-millionaires have been created since launch.

⇨ One in every 24,737 adults is a National Lottery millionaire jackpot winner.[1]

⇨ Over 11,000 people[2] have now banked a life-enhancing prize in excess of £100,000 on the National Lottery's range of draw-based games.

⇨ Around one in every 4,300 people[1] has won a National Lottery prize worth £100,000 or more.

⇨ One in 4 jackpot winners has given away over 30% of their winnings, while 1 in 7 jackpot winners has given £1 million or

Camelot
Serving the nation's dreams

more to a family member or friend – indirectly creating an additional 728 millionaires in 10 years.[3]

⇨ 98% of winners are as happy or happier since hitting the jackpot.[3]

⇨ One in four National Lottery jackpots is won by a syndicate.

Sales

⇨ The National Lottery is currently experiencing the longest period of continuous sales growth in its history.

⇨ Now in their third full year of consecutive growth, in 2005/6, annual National Lottery ticket sales rose by £246 million to hit £5 billion – the biggest yearly increase in eight years.

⇨ The UK National Lottery is ranked fifth in the world by total sales but 58th by per capita spend.[4]

⇨ This means that the majority of National Lottery sales come from a lot of people spending relatively

small amounts – the average weekly spend for all National Lottery games is just under £3.

Breakdown of the lottery pound

⇨ Averaged over the seven-year licence period, out of every £1 spent on National Lottery products 50% is paid out to players in prizes, 28% is contributed to the Good Causes, 12% goes to the Government in lottery duty, 5% covers retailer commission, and 4.5% is retained by Camelot in operating costs, with a further 0.5% returned to its shareholders.

⇨ For every £1 that Camelot makes in profit, £10 goes to retailers, £24 to the Government, £56 to the Good Causes and £100 is paid out to National Lottery players in prize money.

The 2012 Olympic and Paralympic Games in London

⇨ National Lottery funding will contribute up to £1.5 billion towards the costs of staging the 2012 Olympic and Paralympic Games in London.

⇨ Of this, £750 million will come from a series of designated lottery games,[5] like Dream Number – the first draw-based lottery game in support of London 2012 – some National Lottery scratchcards, and online Instant Win Games available at www.national-lottery.co.uk

⇨ Up to the end of September 2006, £53.9 million had been raised for the Olympic Distribution Fund (OLDF) through sales of designated lottery games – £2.3 million ahead of the £14 million target for the first year.

Participation

⇨ The National Lottery has a greater reach than any other consumer product in the UK – around 70% of adults play on a regular basis.

⇨ More than 96% of the UK population either live or work within two miles of a lottery terminal.

Efficiency

⇨ Run on around 4.5% of total revenues, the UK National Lottery is the most cost-efficient lottery in Europe.

⇨ The UK National Lottery is one of the world's most operationally efficient lotteries. Camelot's IT systems have always exceeded the standards set by its regulator, with current availability to sell lottery products at 99.99%.

Leading UK brand

⇨ The National Lottery crossed-fingers logo is instantly recognisable to 95% of the UK population.

⇨ At over £5 billion, annual National Lottery sales are more than £1 billion greater than the combined annual sales of Coca-Cola, Walkers Crisps, Warburton Bread, Cadbury Dairy Milk, Nescafé Coffee, Müller Yogurt, Kingsmill Bread, Hovis Bread, Andrex Toilet Tissue and Robinson's Soft Drinks.[6]

⇨ Buying lottery tickets is the primary reason for visiting a convenience store on a Wednesday, Friday and Saturday for 16% of shoppers[7] – second only to purchasing a newspaper at 18%.

Notes

1 Based on share of the total adult (16+ player) population of the UK of 47 million – Source: Census Day 2001 (29 April)

2 Up to and including the draws on Saturday 6 May 2006, 11,007 players have won prizes in excess of £100,000 on the National Lottery's draw-based games – this figure excludes prizes won on National Lottery Scratchcards.

3 Source: Research conducted by MORI (Market & Opinion Research International) among 86 National Lottery publicity winners, who have won around £1 million or more (Sept-Oct 2004).

4 Source: La Fleur's 2006 World Lottery Almanac.

5 The remaining £340 million will come from the Sports Lottery Fund, and, if needed, up to £410 million from mainstream National Lottery games from 2009.

6 Source: Top 100 Grocery Brands – *Checkout* magazine, March 2005; National Lottery sales figures from Camelot.

7 Source: CTP (Convenience Tracking Programme) – Harris International Marketing

All figures quoted are correct as of October 2006. Camelot Group plc is the licensed operator of The National Lottery® and the crossed-fingers logo is the trademark of the National Lottery Commission.

⇨ The above information is reprinted with kind permission from Camelot. Visit www.camelotgroup. co.uk for more information.

© Camelot

Lottery timeline

Information from the National Lottery Commission

25 October 1993 The Office of the National Lottery (OFLOT) established

25 May 1994 Camelot Group plc selected to run the first UK National Lottery

19 November 1994 First National Lottery draw took place

21 March 1995 Launch of Scratchcards

5 February 1997 Launch of the midweek draw

January 1999 National Lottery Commissioners announced

1 April 1999 The National Lottery Commission succeeded the Office of the National Lottery (OFLOT). Mark Harris appointed as the Commission's Chief Executive

29 July 1999 Statement of Main Principles and timeframe for second Licence competition announced

30 November 1999 Final Invitation to Apply (ITA) and revised draft Licence published

13 November 2000 Launch of Lotto Extra

19 December 2000 Camelot awarded the second seven-year licence

26 October 2001 The interim licence took effect

27 January 2002 Start of the second seven-year licence

10 July 2002 Launch of Lotto HotPicks

23 October 2002 The first midweek Thunderball draw took place

24 February 2003 Launch of Interactive Instant Win Games

22 September 2003 Launch of Daily Play

13 February 2004 Launch of EuroMillions

16 November 2004 First National Lottery Day

25 November 2004 National Lottery Bill introduced to the House of Commons

27 January 2005 The National Lottery Commission publishes its consultation on the third Licence competition, *A Lottery for the Future*

6 July 2005 The International Olympic Committee (IOC) announces decision to award the 2012 Olympic Games to London

8 November 2005 Publication of the Statement of Main Principles for the third Licence competition

28 April 2006 Publication of the Draft Invitation to Apply (ITA) and Draft Licence.

⇨ The above information is reprinted with kind permission from the National Lottery Commission. Visit www.natlotcomm.gov.uk for more information.

© National Lottery Commission

Under 16s and the National Lottery

Research study conducted for the National Lottery Commission – executive summary

Introduction

The 2006 *Under 16s and the National Lottery* study was carried out by MORI Social Research Institute and the International Gaming Research Unit at Nottingham Trent University on behalf of the National Lottery Commission. The research consisted of a quantitative survey of young people aged between 12 and 15 in England and Wales.

This research study follows earlier surveys conducted in 1997, 1999 and 2000 which also examined underage gambling among this age group, using a similar quantitative survey methodology.

Please note that, throughout the report, reference is made to 'problem' and 'social' gamblers. Problem gambling, or pathological gambling, is defined by the American Psychiatric Association as 'persistent and recurrent maladaptive gambling behaviour that disrupts personal, family, or vocational pursuits', gambling that becomes a compulsion despite the negative consequences it causes. Social gambling is defined as, 'gambling which lasts for a limited amount of time with predetermined acceptable losses'. The survey uses the DSM-IV-MR-J screen to identify whether respondents who gamble are problem or social gamblers. Further details of this screen can be found in Section 6 of *Under 16s and the National Lottery – Final Report*, Problem Gambling in young people.

Key findings

⇨ Overall participation in gambling activities by young people under the age of 16 has fallen, both in terms of games they may have *ever* played for money and in the *past year*. This continues the trend identified in previous surveys of declining levels of underage gambling.

National Lottery Commission

⇨ Fruit machines remain the most popular form of underage gambling with over half of young people (54%) saying they have *ever* played on them and 49% in the past year. Boys, those who are older, young people with higher weekly incomes, those who have played truant, those who have taken illegal substances or have parents who gamble, are all more likely to have *ever* gambled for money and to have done so in the *past year*.

⇨ Looking specifically at the National Lottery draw games and Scratchcards the data suggest that underage participation in both forms of gambling has declined since the last survey in 2000. Even with the launch of several new products since 2000, past-week participation in National Lottery draw games taken as a whole has declined from 11% to seven per cent and Scratchcard play has fallen from nine per cent to six per cent. The rate of playing

---

Fruit machines remain the most popular form of underage gambling with over half of young people (54%) saying they have ever played on them and 49% in the past year

---

the main National Lottery draw (Lotto) has declined from 8% to 5% since 2000. However, the amount players spend on each game, and particularly Lotto, has increased. Lotto spending is now in line with spending on fruit machines and higher than

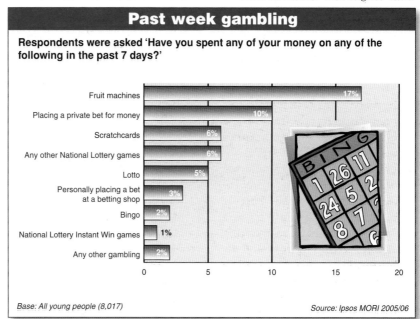

Past week gambling

Respondents were asked 'Have you spent any of your money on any of the following in the past 7 days?'

Fruit machines	17%
Placing a private bet for money	10%
Scratchcards	6%
Any other National Lottery games	6%
Lotto	5%
Personally placing a bet at a betting shop	3%
Bingo	2%
National Lottery Instant Win games	1%
Any other gambling	2%

Base: All young people (8,017)

Source: Ipsos MORI 2005/06

spending on Scratchcards for the first time. To some extent, this reflects typical purchasing behaviour that is also evident in adults: as the number of players of each game decreases, the average amount spent increases, as only the core players remain. However, it might also suggest that while new National Lottery games are not encouraging first-time players, they may be encouraging existing gamblers to play even more games.

⇨ Shops are the most popular retail outlets for young people who purchase National Lottery game tickets and Scratchcards, followed by supermarkets. Indeed three-quarters of past-week gamblers playing National Lottery games or Scratchcards purchased their tickets from a shop or supermarket. The findings do, however, indicate that young people living in coastal areas have other purchasing outlets available to them in addition to shops and supermarkets.

Three-quarters of young people trying to buy Lotto tickets had been refused a sale during the past week (75%) as were half of those trying to purchase Scratchcards (50%)

⇨ Around one-fifth of Lotto and other National Lottery draw game[1] players (17% and 22% respectively) purchased tickets via digital/electronic means in the past week, although the majority of online play appears to focus on playing free trial games or playing with parental supervision.[2] A very small proportion of young people (0.3%) claim to have played National Lottery games on the Internet independently and for money, reflecting the rigorous security settings to prevent access by underage players. For other National Lottery games,

Young people and the National Lottery

Respondents were asked 'Please tell us whether you have ever played the following games for money . . . any National Lottery or scratchcard game'

Category	Percentage
Total	35%
Boys	39%
Girls	30%
12 years of age	30%
15 years of age	40%
Weekly income of up to £10	27%
Weekly income of £30+	51%
Played truant in past year	53%
Taken illegal substances in past year	40%

Base: All young people (8,107) *Source: Ipsos MORI 2005-06*

young people defined as problem gamblers are more likely than those defined as social gamblers to have played games online in the past week.

⇨ Sales of Lotto tickets and Scratchcards to young people under the age of 16 are as likely to be legal as illegal[3] – this represents a slight change from previous surveys when the balance was in favour of legal purchasing. However, sales of other National Lottery draw games are more likely to be legal than illegal. The most common way for young people to acquire tickets and Scratchcards are through purchasing themselves or through their parents buying tickets for them. Older and more affluent children are slightly more likely to purchase tickets themselves than younger children and those with low disposable incomes.

⇨ In the week prior to the survey nine per cent of young people either tried to or did buy a National Lottery draw ticket, and eight per cent either tried to or did buy a Scratchcard. This is similar to the proportions who actually played each type of game – most of those who attempted to purchase tickets managed to do so. However, three-quarters of young people trying to buy Lotto tickets had been refused a sale during the past week (75%) as were half of those trying to purchase

Scratchcards (50%). The findings suggest that, while retailers are being more vigilant in refusing to sell tickets to underage customers (particularly in relation to draw game tickets), there are still inconsistencies between different retail outlets which enable persistent gamblers ultimately to find willing retailers.

⇨ The profile of attempted and refused Scratchcard and National Lottery players is similar to the profile of actual players. However, the key difference between those who were refused tickets and those who managed to purchase tickets, perhaps not unsurprisingly, is age: younger respondents had more problems trying to buy tickets than older children.

⇨ Relatively few young people have ever played a National Lottery game on the Internet – only eight per cent have done so. It should be noted, however, that around one in five Lotto and other National Lottery draw game players have purchased tickets via electronic or digital means.

⇨ Young people who have played a game on the Internet tend to be classified as 'problem gamblers' and have access to more money (£10.00 or more a week). Furthermore, the survey findings suggest that those who play games on the Internet are most likely to be playing Instant Win games (either free or for money) and they are more likely to play with their parents or with their permission than independently.

⇨ Prevalence of overall problem gambling, and the characteristics and behaviours associated with it, has decreased considerably since the previous survey took place in 2000 (from 4.9% then to 3.5% in 2006). Boys are more likely than girls to be problem gamblers and prevalence of problem gambling rises with increasing disposable income. Overall prevalence of problem gambling amongst those who had gambled in the last year was six per cent, of which five per cent only gambled on fruit machines, and 0.5% only gambled on Scratchcards.

Boys are more likely than girls to be problem gamblers and prevalence of problem gambling rises with increasing disposable income

---

⇨ Young people's playing habits in the past seven days tend to mirror their perceptions of what their parents have played over the same time period with a few obvious exceptions: the most popular games played by young people tend to be easier to access or involve private bets with friends, while their parents are more likely to have played National Lottery games.

⇨ In the final section of the survey we explored young people's views on gambling and found that the majority of young people agree that gambling can lead to addiction, that gambling is not a good thing for someone their age to be spending money on and that playing National Lottery draw games can lead to serious debt issues. However, when asked about Scratchcards opinion is somewhat mixed, with young people divided over whether playing Scratchcards can lead to overspending and debt.

About the study

The 2006 study into Under 16s and the National Lottery set out to measure and assess the motivations for and prevalence of gambling among 12- to 15-year-olds. Specifically the survey set out to update the research last conducted with young people in 2000, measure current levels of underage gambling among the 12- to 15-year-old age group, identify key socio-demographics trends of those who play the National Lottery, compare levels of underage gambling on the National Lottery with underage participation in other forms of gambling, and assess under 16s' attitudes towards gambling.

In order to meet the aims and objectives outlined above, a survey of 8,017 young people aged between 12 and 15 years of age was carried out through interviewer-administered paper self-completion sessions in classroom lessons. This is the same data collection method as used in all previous studies. Fieldwork for the study was conducted between 26th September 2005 and 10th February 2006. Full details of the research design and approach to sampling can be found in the Appendices of the main report.

Notes

1 'Other' National Lottery draw games includes all National Lottery draw games except Lotto: Lotto Extra, Lotto HotPicks, Thunderball, Daily Play, and EuroMillions.

2 Among the 8% of respondents who say they have played National Lottery games on the Internet, 29% said they played free games, 29% say they played with their parents or with their parents' permission, 35% said they could not remember, and 22% said they had played independently.

3 Legal sales are defined as sales to adults aged 16 or above, even if purchases are made on behalf of someone under 16. If a young person under the age of 16 purchases a ticket themselves, the sale is deemed to be illegal.

June 2006

⇨ An extract from the report *Under 16s and the National Lottery – Final Report*, conducted by Ipsos MORI on behalf of the National Lottery Commission, and is reprinted with permission. Visit www.natlotcomm. gov.uk for more information or to view the full report.

© *Ipsos MORI/National Lottery Commission*

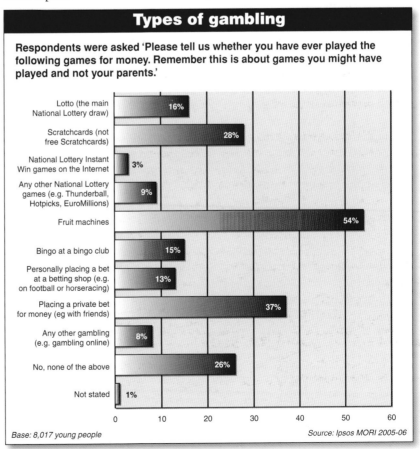

Types of gambling

Respondents were asked 'Please tell us whether you have ever played the following games for money. Remember this is about games you might have played and not your parents.'

Type	%
Lotto (the main National Lottery draw)	16%
Scratchcards (not free Scratchcards)	28%
National Lottery Instant Win games on the Internet	3%
Any other National Lottery games (e.g. Thunderball, Hotpicks, EuroMillions)	9%
Fruit machines	54%
Bingo at a bingo club	15%
Personally placing a bet at a betting shop (e.g. on football or horseracing)	13%
Placing a private bet for money (eg with friends)	37%
Any other gambling (e.g. gambling online)	8%
No, none of the above	26%
Not stated	1%

Base: 8,017 young people   Source: Ipsos MORI 2005-06

UK's first supercasino

Originally, there were to be 40 supercasinos. Now there will be just one. We look at Britain's biggest gamble...

Vegas comes to the UK

By the end of 2006, the UK will know the location of its first supercasino. In December, the Casino Advisory Panel, an independent body, will decide from a shortlist of eight where the supercasino is to be located.

The supercasino will be a vast Vegas-style 'pleasure palace' that accommodates 1,250 slot machines, with jackpots of up to £1 million. The country's current 140 casinos have no more than 10 slots each and four-figure jackpots.

The panel will also decide the location of eight 'large' casinos and eight 'small' casinos. The large casinos will offer up to 150 slots with jackpots up to £4,000. The small casinos will have up to 80 slots.

Forty to one

These plans, radical enough in a country still gambling under legislation made nearly 40 years ago, are actually a watering down of the government's original intentions for 40 supercasinos.

Having just one supercasino to scrap over is a disappointment for the eight councils who are bidding.

Some see a supercasino as a shortcut to reviving economically downtrodden areas. After all, the US gambling firms who originally dangled the idea of supercasinos

By James Lamb

in front of government ministers claimed that up to 100,000 new jobs could be created.

> **The supercasino will be a vast Vegas-style 'pleasure palace' that accommodates 1,250 slot machines, with jackpots of up to £1 million**

The scaling down of casino plans means that jobs' figure won't be reached, but economic benefits are still anticipated. In shortlisted Cardiff, the council see the supercasino as a catalyst for the development of an 80-acre sports village on the waterfront.

Taking a gamble

So who could argue against a Vegas-style experience that helps regenerate urban areas? Well, the Church of Scotland and the Salvation Army to name but two. They are concerned that a supercasino could lead to an increase in problem gambling.

Indeed, research in the US has shown that six per cent of people living near supercasinos become gambling addicts. Reacting to the concerns, Culture Secretary Tessa Jowell has said that she will shut casinos if there's an increase in problem gambling.

Keeping an eye on the prize

Then again, Professor Peter Collins at Salford University's Centre for the Study of Gambling, claims supercasinos lead to fewer problem gamblers as long as there is investment in public awareness campaigns about the dangers.

GamCare, the gambling advice charity, will be keeping a close eye on things – the total number of people approaching it for counselling rose by 41.3% to 6,563 in 2005.

Then there are those who ignore the moral and sociological arguments, but contend that as the supercasino is to be located in a less salubrious area it's unlikely to provide the tourist attraction cash cow the government is hoping for. It seems the supercasino is a big gamble even before it's built.

⇨ The above information is reprinted with kind permission from virgin.net. Visit www.virgin.net for more information.

© virgin.net

Q&A: Supercasino

The shortlist of venues has been released for Britain's first supercasino, but will the enterprise have a positive effect on the wider community? Matthew Weaver weighs up the odds

What is it?

An all-day Las Vegas-style gambling palace, which will be allowed to include 1,250 slot machines with a jackpot of £1m, under the government's new Gambling Act.

Sometimes it is referred to as mega-casino or regional-casino. It is not to be confused with a new generation of large casinos, which will have the right to operate 150 machines with jackpots of £5,000, under the act.

How many will there be?

The government originally said there could be as many as 40 supercasinos and an unlimited number of large casinos. But controversy about the idea forced ministers into retreat over the numbers.

There is a worry that the new casinos will increase gambling addiction

---

First the number of supercasinos was cut to just eight – one for each region. Then, in a last-ditch attempt to get the new gambling measures through parliament, culture minister Tessa Jowell cut the number to just one.

A limit of eight has also been placed on the number of large casinos, with eight smaller versions also to be built, bringing the total number of new casinos to 17.

Where will the supercasino be built?

The independent casino advisory panel today released a shortlist of eight council areas.

They are: Blackpool, Brent (Wembley Stadium), Cardiff, Glasgow, Greenwich (the Millennium Dome), Manchester, Newcastle and Shef-field. The panel will now choose a single venue by the end of the year. London's Millennium Dome, Blackpool, Glasgow and Manchester are the favourites to host the supercasino.

Which councils failed to make today's list?

Chesterfield, Coventry, Dartford, Dudley, Great Yarmouth, Havering, Hull, Ipswich, Leeds, Middlesbrough, Midlothian, Newport, Solihull, Southampton, Southend-on-Sea, Sunderland, Thurrock, Wakefield and West Dunbartonshire.

What about the 16 smaller casinos?

The panel also announced a shortlist of 31 proposals for large and small casinos.

They are: Bath & North East Somerset, Bournemouth, Brighton, Canterbury, Chelmsford, Dartford, Dudley, Dumfries and Galloway, East Lindsey, Great Yarmouth, Hastings, Hull, Leeds, Leicester, Luton, Mansfield, Middlesbrough, Milton Keynes, Newham, North East Lincolnshire, Peterborough, Restormel, Scarborough, Sefton, Solihull, Southampton, South Tyneside, Swansea, Thurrock, Torbay and Wolverhampton.

How did the panel select the shortlist?

The selection was made against a set of criteria, which include the social and regeneration impacts on the area.

Why have the new casinos been introduced?

US gambling firms persuaded ministers that new casinos could create up to 100,000 new jobs and help regenerate run-down areas.

The original idea was to attract investment by freeing up Britain's prudish gambling laws. But the measures have been so watered down that they now amount to little more than a tightly controlled experiment.

Why is the idea so controversial?

Critics fear that the proposals will increase crime and lead to trashy new development.

There is also a worry that the new casinos will increase gambling addiction, which is already on the rise. Gambling advice charity GamCare said today that the total number of people approaching it for counselling rose 41.3% to 6,563 in 2005 from the previous year.

What happens if those fears are realised?

The new casinos will be reviewed after three years. Culture secretary Tessa Jowell insists she will shut down casinos if it was shown they were increasing gambling problems.

Who is against new casinos?

Concerns have been voiced from both the right and left, notably in both the *Daily Mail* and the *Guardian*. Church groups and charities are some of the most vocal opponents.

What about existing casinos?

The British owners of the existing 140 casinos were relieved that the government has acted to limit the number of new gambling dens. They had feared being forced out of business by the American operators of the larger casinos.

Under the new laws existing casinos will be allowed to double the number of slot machines from 10 to 20, with maximum jackpots of £4,000. They will also be allowed to operate without membership restrictions for punters.

24 May 2006

Risks of the 'supercasino'

Gambling on the risks posed by Britain's first 'supercasino'

By Julia Kollewe

Today (14 August) is the deadline for local authorities to submit their final proposals for the siting of Britain's first Las Vegas-style casino. However, plans for the new supercasino, with up to 1,250 slot machines and unlimited jackpots, have attracted controversy.

First, the Government was forced to whittle down its original plans for eight supercasinos to just one after an outcry from gambling addiction charities and Labour backbenchers. Then in May the shortlist of possible locations was met with cries of outrage when bids from Coventry, Birmingham and Dudley were omitted, while Blackpool, Wembley Stadium, Cardiff, Glasgow, Greenwich, Manchester, Newcastle and Sheffield were all included.

As of autumn 2007, gambling operators will be able to advertise in all media

When the Millennium Dome emerged as the official frontrunner for the licence last month, further issues were raised over Deputy Prime Minister John Prescott's alleged links with the developer of the Greenwich site.

Amid the threat of legal action from the local authorities left off the shortlist, the Casino Advisory Panel extended the deadline for them to make further submissions to today. However, the Panel's chairman Professor Stephen Crow said he was concerned that not all authorities may have been aware of this opportunity.

After visiting each of the shortlisted sites, the Panel will make a recommendation to Culture Secretary Tessa Jowell by mid-December, and Parliament will get the final say on the winning location early 2007.

Gambling is becoming an increasingly mainstream pastime. Over a third of Britons bet on the Grand National, the country's single biggest gambling event. More women and younger people have flocked to casinos since the 24-hour rule was scrapped last October, which means punters can now sign up at the door and start gambling immediately.

Last year Britons staked £66bn on gambling, according to the consumer research firm Mintel – up from £25bn in 2001 when the Government started the biggest shake-up of the gambling laws since the 1960s. In addition to the supercasino, this will allow for eight new large casinos and eight small ones to be built. Also, as of autumn 2007, gambling operators will be able to advertise in all media.

However, the number of problems associated with gambling is growing – especially as the recent boom in on-line poker, casino and sportsbetting sites has resulted in round-the-clock betting. In response to this, the ESRC is funding a new research venture in partnership with the Responsibility in Gambling Trust (RIGT).

A spokesperson from RIGT said the venture would 'help us to understand why people become involved in gambling, how people learn to control their addiction, and how we can prevent people from becoming problem gamblers'.

While councils are vying for the supercasino licence, which they hope will kick-start the local economy, many people are worried about the social impact. In a recent poll of Londoners, nearly half opposed a supercasino in the capital, while only a third backed it.

Already two ESRC-funded projects are considering some of the less welcome knock-on effects of gambling. Dr Stephanie Van Goozen from Cardiff University is looking at the link between young males' problem gambling and drug taking, drunkenness, risky sexual behaviour and employment problems. She says, 'It's important to have an appreciation of the relationship between problem gambling and more serious activities.'

In another ongoing study, Dr Rebecca Cassidy, from Goldsmith's College in London, is studying problem gambling and the capital's betting shops. She says: 'In order to understand what goes wrong when gambling negatively impacts people's lives it is first necessary to understand what gambling means to them and to their families and communities.'

Dr Cassidy's project will culminate in an international conference, which it is hoped will bring together new approaches to the problem drawn from across the world.

14 August 2006

⇨ The above information is reprinted with kind permission from the Economic and Social Research Council. Visit www.esrc.ac.uk for more information.

Interactive or remote gambling

An extract from *Gambling or Gaming: Entertainment or Exploitation?*

Interactive or remote gambling covers gambling via Internet, mobile handsets and television. The government reports that most of the recent gambling review will now regulate remote gambling, an activity which specialists suggest 80,000 adults participate in each month. The traditional methods of gambling are increasingly being augmented with electronic forms of gambling, most notably from the Internet where newly launched companies are increasing the profile of gambling, such as www.888.com. Even the traditional gambling companies have Internet gambling facilities, such as betting online with www.williamhill.co.uk and the National Lottery.

£5bn a year is wagered online with 93% of people with Internet access having gambled on the web

The Remote Gambling Association published a code of practice on social responsibility and age verification at the end of 2005. This is welcome in light of the limited and weak controls via the Internet to prevent underage gambling that currently appear in place.

Online gambling
The Online Gambling Market Research Handbook, an industry report, cited future revenues of the online gambling industry could dwarf other Internet services. The average casino keeps around 75% of monies deposited, which has caused some analysts in the market to estimate the business's worth will be US$12bn by 2015.

The 1968 Gaming Act does not cover Internet gambling sites in Great Britain for obvious reasons. The Act requires casinos to be premises-based and those who wish to gamble must attend these licensed premises. Companies offering Internet gambling to UK residents must have their servers and other gambling facilities based off-shore to avoid contravening the law in the UK. However, the 2005 Gambling Act provides for Internet casinos to be based in Great Britain and regulated by the Gambling Commission. This Act however has not come into effect yet, so for the time being, it is still illegal to base Internet gambling sites in the UK. However, this poses some problems, for instance it means that these companies are not subject to UK law and are therefore outside the jurisdiction of the Gambling Commission. If there are problems facing British customers, there is little the Gambling Commission can do to intervene.

The law does not however make it illegal to participate in gambling activities via the Internet in Britain. The advertising laws on promoting Internet gambling are very tight and would, in the Gambling Commission's view, allow little more than the publication of the name of the site. In November 2005, the BBC reported that Culture Secretary Tessa Jowell plans to prevent gambling companies from advertising free entry to online tournaments or indicate the value of prizes, following accusations that companies were flouting laws that prevented casinos from offering inducements to gamble.

The online gambling market in the UK is growing rapidly and despite the restrictions in terms of what can be advertised, UK online casinos and poker rooms are increasing their advertising with huge sports sponsorship and poster advertising. The top ten UK gambling or sweepstake sites are the National Lottery (35%), William Hill (6.3%), Partypoker.com (6.2%), Ladbrokes (5.6%), Pacific Poker (4%), Cyberslotz (3.7%), the Gaming Club (3.5%), LoopyLotto (3.2%), Golden Palace Online Casino (3.1%) and Vernons (2.7%). £5bn a year is wagered online with 93% of people with Internet access having gambled on the web. The average spend per week on gaming sites is between £10 and £20. Online football receives £1bn in wagers, with £835m on Internet casinos, £665m on horse racing and £42m on poker sites.

Online gambling provides the ability to gamble 24 hours a day from the safety of your own home. Associated problems include the increased risk of exposure and access to children and the absorption to computers in terms of time.

New ways of tapping into the Internet gambling market are constantly being sought. For example, Ryanair recently announced plans to introduce in-flight gambling, with the hope eventually of being able to offer free flights to all passengers as it generates its income from gambling.

One of the more worrying aspects of online gambling is perhaps the ability for those under the legal age to access sites that provide gambling facilities. A report by Lancaster University suggests that most children can access online gambling sites. Some sites, such as the National Lottery and Ladbrokes, have means of blocking access to underage gambling; however, it appears that the majority of sites do not have effective screening tools and blocking technology. The majority of online payment methods are only available to those over 18 years of age. Children do, however, have access to various types of payment cards, such as Visa Electron debit cards, that may be used to fund gambling. The Remote Gambling Association encourages its members to focus efforts on preventing these types of payments from underage gamblers. The Code requires certain checks and verification procedures, which will go some way to helping prevent underage gambling.

Gambling services by mobile handset are a relatively new phenomenon

---

Gambling via mobile

Gambling services by mobile handset are a relatively new phenomenon with some analysts predicting that this is what the mobile telephone companies have been waiting for, predicting that it could grow into a multi-million-pound business as part of the adult-to-mobile services on offer. The growth of the mobile market, the desire for lotteries, and an increasing awareness of interactive gambling may mean that the number of gambling services mobile phones offer could explode. This could also mean powerful partnerships between mobile phone operators desperate to claw back some of the investment into new technology, and gambling companies looking to increase their market share. Although some estimate that lotteries will be the most successful of all forms of mobile

gambling services, accounting for around 40% of all mobile gambling revenues by 2009, other forms of gambling could be driven to rapid growth by the service providers.

Gambling via a mobile handset is incredibly easy. It takes up to a day to register and set up an online account. Once this is done, the user is then able to download his preferred java-enabled gambling application on to the handset, browse games and the odds, and place bets at a press of a button. The money is immediately debited from the user's account. With the ability to be invoiced

through your phone bill, there is the possibility of concealing what the user is spending their money on. *March 2006*

⇨ An extract from the Church of England's Ethical Advisory Group's document, *Gambling or Gaming: Entertainment or Exploitation?*, reprinted with permission of the Archbishops' Council. Please visit http://www.cofe.anglican.org/info/ethical/policystatements/gambling.pdf to view the full text of this report.
© *Ethical Investment Advisory Group of the Church of England*

Are there any benefits to gambling?

An extract from *Gambling or Gaming: Entertainment or Exploitation?*

Tax revenues

It is easy to see that an industry that is estimated to be worth around £63bn a year would be an attractive form of fiscal revenue for the government. Opening up the gambling industry will inevitably increase revenues from this already lucrative source.

However, some are concerned that the desire for increased tax revenues is driving changes devoid of any concern for the social wellbeing of the public at large, with particular concern about gambling-related problems such as addiction, indebtedness and breakdown of family life.

Social activity

Gambling is often carried out in a social context, which provides entertainment and often safe venues in which to enjoy an evening out with friends, such as bingo. In this social context, many people enjoy the thrill and excitement a day at the races or a night at a casino provides.

There is also the social benefit of raising money through lotteries for a social or sporting club or local community initiative.

Good causes

The introduction of the National Lottery has shifted public perceptions of gambling. It has provided a great stream of revenue for good causes, as already discussed.

However, some charities and local sports groups have complained that since its introduction, their revenues have fallen drastically.
March 2006

⇨ The above information is an extract from the Church of England's Ethical Advisory Groups document, *Gambling or Gaming: Entertainment or Exploitation?*, and is reprinted with permission of the Archbishops' Council. Please visit http://www.cofe.anglican.org/info/ethical/policystatements/gambling.pdf to view the full text of this report.
© *Ethical Investment Advisory Group of the Church of England*

Boom in online gambling

Online gambling will continue to prosper in the UK, a new report has revealed

UK spending on Internet gambling will increase by a whopping 142 per cent to reach £1.6bn by 2010, according to industry analysts Research and Markets.

The number of online gamblers in the UK will grow from 1.1m to 2.1m over the next four years

British consumers spent £660m on Internet gambling sites in 2005.

The report also predicts that the number of online gamblers in the UK will grow from 1.1m to 2.1m over the next four years.

'Strong growth in UK consumer spending on online gambling from 2000 was initially generated by predominantly "hard core" gamblers,' the report said.

By Nick Gibbens

'However, future growth will be driven by more leisure-oriented consumers from 2006 as demonstrated by the emergence and growth of simpler gambling formats targeting the mass market, in particular gaming and lotto.

'For the first time gambling products are competing with other forms of mass entertainment for consumer attention and spending'

'For the first time gambling products are competing with other forms of mass entertainment for consumer attention and spending.'

Research and Markets said the report was essential reading for online gambling operators, industry investors, technology providers and sub-contractors as well as media companies looking to generate revenues from broadband services.

In March 2006, London-based interactive betting company Leisure & Gaming reported 2005 profits of £24.1m.

Partygaming, the world's largest online gaming operator, has also enjoyed a bumper period. The Gibraltar-based group saw revenues climb 50 per cent to £172.7m in the three months to the end of June.

The promising results come amid growing fears of a crackdown on Internet gambling in the US.

Earlier this month, the US House of Representatives approved a bill that would ban most forms of online gambling and make it illegal for banks and credit card firms to make payments to Internet gambling operators.

25 July 2006

⇨ The above information is reprinted with kind permission from 999Today. For more informaion, please visit their website at www.999today.com

© 999Today

Gambling and sweepstake sites

Top 10 UK gambling/sweepstake sites (gambling/sweepstakes sector reach)

Site	percentage
The National Lottery	35%
William Hill	6.3%
Party-poker.com	6.2%
Ladbrokes	5.6%
Pacific Poker	4%
Cyber-slotz	3.7%
The Gaming Club	3.5%
Loopy Lotto	3.2%
Golden Palace Online Casino	3.1%
Vernons	2.7%

Source: Nielsen//NetRatings. UK home only data, February 2005

Online gambling in Europe

More than 14 million Europeans fancy a flutter online

The latest research from Nielsen//NetRatings, the Internet research specialists, reveals that more than 14 million Europeans, or 14% of those online from home, visited a gambling and sweepstakes site in February. Gambling and sweepstakes sites were most popular with French and Swedish surfers, but have yet to make a mark in southern Europe, with less than 10% of Spanish and Italians logging on to gamble.

In all the countries under measurement across Europe, the majority of visitors to gambling and sweepstakes sites are using a high-speed Internet connection. France, Switzerland and Spain lead the way with more than 80% of visitors to online gambling sites connecting via broadband.

What we normally see in the majority of categories is that the high-speed users spend the greatest amount of time online. For gambling and sweepstakes sites, however, this is not always the case. In France, Sweden and the UK, the time spent on gambling and sweepstakes sites is very similar, suggesting that slower connection speed is not offputting for the determined gamblers in these countries. By comparison, in Switzerland, Italy and Germany high-speed Internet users are spending significantly more time than those connecting at a slower speed.

In the UK, the National Lottery is the most popular gambling and sweepstakes site, with over 1.3 million visitors from home in February 2005. This audience figure puts the site in the top 40 most visited sites in the UK. The gambling category in the UK has seen strong growth over the past twelve months, with audiences up by 45% when compared to the same time last year. This growth has been driven by a range of gambling, betting and online casino sites, and not just by the National Lottery, which appeals to specific demographic groups, and is a lottery-based site rather than a full online betting or gambling site.

Gabrielle Prior, European Internet Analyst, says: 'With more than one in ten online Europeans visiting a gambling site this is clearly an important sector for the Internet industry. Online gambling and casino sites are also prolific online and offline advertisers. We expect to see this category continue to grow as advertising attracts consumers and the sites add more and more games and prizes. We know from earlier survey work that UK gamblers like the speed and convenience of betting online, and as the broadband boom continues we expect more people to try online gambling.'
14 April 2005

⇨ The above information is reprinted with kind permission from Nielsen//NetRatings. Visit www.nielsen-netratings.com for more information.

© *Nielsen//NetRatings*

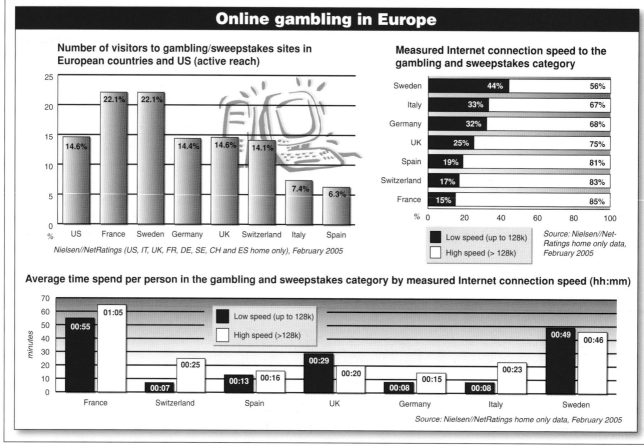

Online gambling in Europe

Number of visitors to gambling/sweepstakes sites in European countries and US (active reach)

US 14.6% • France 22.1% • Sweden 22.1% • Germany 14.4% • UK 14.6% • Switzerland 14.1% • Italy 7.4% • Spain 6.3%

Nielsen//NetRatings (US, IT, UK, FR, DE, SE, CH and ES home only), February 2005

Measured Internet connection speed to the gambling and sweepstakes category

Country	Low speed (up to 128k)	High speed (> 128k)
Sweden	44%	56%
Italy	33%	67%
Germany	32%	68%
UK	25%	75%
Spain	19%	81%
Switzerland	17%	83%
France	15%	85%

Source: Nielsen//NetRatings home only data, February 2005

Average time spend per person in the gambling and sweepstakes category by measured Internet connection speed (hh:mm)

France: Low 00:55 / High 01:05
Switzerland: Low 00:07 / High 00:25
Spain: Low 00:13 / High 00:16
UK: Low 00:29 / High 00:20
Germany: Low 00:08 / High 00:15
Italy: Low 00:08 / High 00:23
Sweden: Low 00:49 / High 00:46

Source: Nielsen//NetRatings home only data, February 2005

Online gambling drives addiction rates

Women now making a fifth of calls to gambling addiction helplines

The success of online and mobile gambling has caused a rise in the number of people with gambling addictions and debts, according to a report released today.

GamCare claimed that there are now up to 350,000 people in Britain with a gambling addiction

'The unregulated online and mobile phone gaming services pose the greatest threat,' said Anthony Jennens, chairman of gambling addiction charity GamCare. 'This is the growth market where vulnerable people are falling into difficulties.'

GamCare claimed that there are now up to 350,000 people in Britain with a gambling addiction.

By Matt Chapman

The charity added that six years ago only two per cent of those seeking help were women, compared with nine per cent of those seeking counselling today and 18 per cent of calls received to the GamCare helpline on 0845 6000 133.

The number of women with gambling problems was attributed to the rapid rise of online gambling sites, as women would not previously have visited traditional betting shops.

GamCare also said that its help forum has grown from fewer than 10,000 users nine months ago to more than 90,000 today.

Culture Secretary Tessa Jowell told the BBC's *Today* programme that the recent changes in the gambling laws were designed to regulate the industry.

'One option is unsustainable and that is doing nothing and expecting people to be protected in a modern environment with the Internet and new forms of gambling which were never heard of when the legislation was introduced in 1968,' she said.

Jowell agreed that the uptake of online gambling brought particular risks. 'As things stand it is an explosion over which we have very little control and that is why online gambling will be regulated under the new gambling act,' she said.

The minister added that the government hoped to persuade offshore operators to move their businesses to the UK and become properly recognised.
25 May 2006

⇨ The above information is reprinted with kind permission from vnunet.com. Visit www.vnunet.com for more information.

© *vnunet.com*

Internet betting

How Internet betting can draw you into a web of self-destruction

Internet gamblers are more likely to have a serious gambling problem than others, it is claimed.

GamCare, a charity dealing with the social impact of gambling, said: 'There is an isolation factor, unlike a casino or betting shop where someone can tap you on the shoulder and say, "Are you OK?"'

A spokesman for Gamblers Anonymous UK said that last year there had been 'a surge' of Internet gamblers pleading for help.

'People who have been on the Internet or tried poker online seem to have been doing it for one to three

By Sarah Womack, Social Affairs Correspondent

years before they get into trouble,' said a spokesman.

'I was a bookie and casino gambler and it took me 20 years before I recognised I had a problem.

'The trouble is that the money goes quick because it's on the screen. It's just numbers on a computer; it's not notes in your hand and, of course, Internet gamblers use credit cards.'

In a survey in *Psychology of Addictive Behaviours* journal, Dr

George Ladd and Dr Nancy Petry, psychologists at the University of Connecticut health centre, monitored the gambling behaviour of 389 people.

They found that nearly 11 per cent were problem gamblers and more than 15 per cent met the criteria for pathological gamblers.

Internet gambling was the least common gambling activity of those surveyed but 74 per cent of those who gambled on the web had serious problems.

In Britain doctors have issued a warning that Internet gambling and supercasinos will cause an explosion in gambling addiction.

Dr Vivienne Nathanson, the head of science and ethics at the British Medical Association, said that GPs had already reported seeing more people with gambling addictions. 'If it gets out of control it can tear families apart and cause a whole host of mental and physical problems,' she said.

There is political pressure on credit card firms to place a cap on how much can be spent on Internet gambling sites. Mike Weir, the

---

In Britain doctors have issued a warning that Internet gambling and supercasinos will cause an explosion in gambling addiction

---

Scottish National Party MP for Angus, has called for a limit of £1,000 a week and for sites to limit players to one credit card each.

There are an estimated 2,300 gambling sites on the Internet and about four million people in Britain gamble online every month. That figure is forecast to grow by 22 per cent this year.

The Remote Gambling Association said it had a code of conduct which required its 34 members, which are online betting and poker sites, to have links to problem gambling advice organisations.

They must also have facilities on their websites which allow customers to limit the amount of money they can gamble and to be excluded from the sites for certain periods of time. From next year online gambling based in Britain will be regulated by the Gambling Commission.
11 July 2006

Gambling at work

Information from the Carole Spiers Group

The row in the tabloid newspapers over England striker Wayne Rooney's alleged £700,000 gambling debt, supposedly run up in just six months, has turned the spotlight on the problem of workers who gamble.

Q How big a problem is Internet gambling?
A You may think that gambling is not a problem an employer needs to be worried about, and is just 'a bit

---

By Carole Spiers, business stress consultant

---

of fun' and part of everyday culture. However, online gambling is making it easy for employees to get hooked. According to eMarketer (March 2006), global online gambling revenues reached 6.25bn last year, up 28%. In the UK, 53bn was spent last year on all forms of gambling

(including the National Lottery), with one million people regularly gambling online.

Q What are the telltale signs that an employee is gambling?
A Gambling has been called 'the hidden addiction'. Unlike drug or alcohol addiction, it may be difficult to detect as there are no obvious physical signs of a compulsive gambler. Like other addicts, however, they will typically deny any problem until they are desperate for help.

It is important, therefore, for managers and occupational health practitioners to look out for telltale signs. These might include persistent lateness or absenteeism and excessive use of the telephone or rest rooms.

Among the clearest indications of a serious gambling problem are: borrowing money to bet or pay off debts; any effort to conceal their gambling, as this implies guilt that there is a problem; and the amount of leisure time devoted to gambling.

Before the advent of online gambling, compulsive gamblers might have had poor attendance

records, but it may now be necessary to look for subtler signs such as: only having half their mind on their job; appearing withdrawn and less of a team player; secrecy; reduced productivity; irregular time-keeping; or general capability issues.

Three studies of Gamblers Anonymous members and others in treatment found that roughly two-thirds admitted to committing crimes or fraud to finance their gambling

---

Q How bad can it get?

A Research shows that by the time most compulsive gamblers seek help, they are hugely in debt and their family life is a shambles. About 80% seriously consider suicide, and up to 20% attempt or succeed in killing themselves.

Three studies of Gamblers Anonymous members and others in treatment found that roughly two-thirds admitted to committing crimes or fraud to finance their gambling. In another study, 47% of the Gamblers Anonymous members surveyed admitted to carrying out some form of insurance fraud, embezzlement or arson.

Q What is the government doing?

A The Gambling Act 2005 comes fully into force in September 2007. Proposed new rules governing the future of gambling in the UK were also published by the Gambling Commission in March. They include:

⇨ Operators publishing policies and procedures for promoting 'socially responsible gambling'

⇨ Information and advice for problem gamblers being prominently displayed

⇨ Online operators telling customers how much time and money they are spending on their sites.

Q What are the legal implications of gambling in work time?

A If an employee is gambling in work time they may be in breach of contract if they are not carrying out their duties and employers should use their disciplinary procedure. If the individual is involved in fraud or theft then it could amount to gross misconduct.

Depending on an employer's disciplinary procedure, Internet gambling at work could be viewed as gross misconduct involving the potential misuse of company property, unauthorised Internet use, and the misuse of company time. As individuals get 'sucked in deeper' to this problem they run greater risks and may get involved in breaches of confidentiality, workplace espionage, theft and fraud.

Employers should make it clear in their computer and Internet policies and disciplinary procedure that gambling at work is unacceptable and will be treated as a disciplinary matter.

Q What can managers do?

A If managers suspect an employee is regularly gambling using the Internet, they should talk to the employee about any stress they might be experiencing, as people gamble when they can see no way out, and an early intervention could resolve this. If you find an employee has been gambling online during work hours, use an informal warning. If their work appears to be suffering, you could go down the capability route if the problem persists.

Just as with alcohol or drug addiction, the employer should consider offering support to any employee it suspects is involved in regular gambling, such as an employee assistance programme and debt counselling.

25 April 2006

⇨ Information from the Carole Spiers Group. Visit www.carolespiersgroup.com for more information, or email them on info@carolespiersgroup.co.uk

© *Carole Spiers*

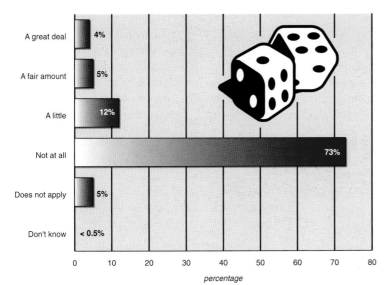

Worrying about gambling

Responses given when asked to what extent, if at all, the respondent had worried about gambling in the last 2-3 weeks.

Response	Percentage
A great deal	4%
A fair amount	5%
A little	12%
Not at all	73%
Does not apply	5%
Don't know	< 0.5%

percentage

Source: Ipsos MORI, 'Britain Today' survey. MORI interviewed 1,001 adults aged 18+ by telephone between 12-17 January 2006. Data are weighted to match the profile of the population. Where percentages do not sum up to 100, this may be due to computer rounding, the exclusion of 'don't know' categories, or multiple answers.

£1m online loser jailed

Judge condemns online gambling as £1m loser is jailed

By Amy Iggulden

A judge attacked the 'staggering' growth of Internet betting sites as he jailed an online gambling addict who stole more than £1 million from his employer.

Bryan Benjafield, 23, an accounts administrator earning £16,000 a year, was yesterday jailed for five years after stealing up to £10,000 a day, forcing his building firm employer to go into liquidation and lay off three staff.

> **'Internet or online gambling has made it much easier, regretfully, for enormous sums to be spent unthinkingly'**

He exploited his position to transfer money to his bank account, then into his Ladbrokes and Skybet Internet account, betting on horse-racing, football matches, Internet poker and other online casino games.

Over 18 months, he siphoned off £1,097,550 from the accounts of Charminster Ltd, a building firm in Dorchester, Dorset, to fund his desktop gambling habits.

He won about £50,000 but lost the equivalent of a tenth of his company's annual turnover.

Benjafield, of Bere Regis, Dorset, who is newly married with a 12-month-old son, admitted obtaining a money transfer by deception, transferring criminal property and two charges of theft.

Judge Andrew Langdon told Dorchester Crown Court that Internet gambling sites, worth more than £12 billion a year globally, had worsened Benjafield's addiction.

'The ease with which a desperate man addicted to gambling could spend enormous sums is bluntly staggering,' he said.

'Internet or online gambling has made it much easier, regretfully, for enormous sums to be spent unthinkingly.' Online gambling is among the fastest-growing Internet industries, with about 2,000 websites operating around the world.

It is currently illegal to run poker and casino betting sites in Britain, but from January firms can apply to set up an infinite number under the Gambling Act 2005, which will come into force in September next year. Online betting for sports is already allowed.

Campaigners fear that the online gambling craze is creating more addicts. It is thought four million people gamble online in Britain each month.

The court heard that Benjafield's boss, Mike Jones, had known him since he was 17 and trusted him so much that within a year of hiring him he had given him access to the company accounts, along with the authority to withdraw cash for wages.

Benjafield's colleagues in the firm's open-plan offices regularly used to see him hunched over his computer screen, believing him to be hard at work, but much of the time he was gambling away the company's money.

Mr Jones, 45, said: 'I have no sympathy for him. He knew what he was doing. It is no good saying he was an addict to excuse what he did.'

The offences came to light after Customs & Excise contacted the company because of an unpaid VAT bill.

An investigation later discovered that large sums of money had been taken from the account used to pay tax bills and it was almost empty.

2 August 2006

Online poker hooks teenagers

Underage gamblers lose thousands as laws fail to keep up

By James Silver

Slumped in front of the flickering screen, Steve has the jaded, world-weary air of a veteran gambler. The trouble is, he's just 17 years old. He says he likes to play on the most popular poker websites because they attract 'all the fish' – the novices and poker also-rans who lose quickly and make easy pickings. Steve has been playing online poker for a year. It is illegal for under-18s, but he found the age verification systems of his chosen websites 'very, very easy' to fool.

He caught the bug after watching big-money tournaments on television. 'I guess I thought the image of guys sitting around a table smoking cigars playing for lots of money was pretty cool,' he says.

Edinburgh-based Steve learnt the basics by staking 'play money' at 'poker school' sites run by the big online poker companies alongside their gambling sites. Within a month, he was betting cash. 'I just typed poker into Google and started playing on the first sites that came up. I deposited money using my own debit card and just registered using a fake date of birth.' So, 18 months on, is he winning? 'Oh yes, definitely, in the long run, but you can have huge swings each week. This week I lost $2,000 [online poker is denominated in dollars], but the week before I won $3,000 (£1,740). Poker's all about skill in the end and I've taken the trouble to learn the game.' Steve intends to postpone university for a year to play 'full time' for 'five or six hours a day'.

But Steve betrays many of the telltale signs of a problem gambler. He says he thinks about poker 'pretty much all the time', gets 'a real buzz' from a good hand of cards, and admits the game distracts him from his college work and social life.

Globally, online poker is worth billions of dollars. Steve, who tells his story in a Radio 4 *Crossing Continents* programme this week, is one of 40 million online gamblers around the world. That number is predicted to quadruple by 2020. It's estimated that in Britain online gamblers stake £3m a day – among them, young players lured by the game's glitzy TV image. The craze has rippled through American universities and high schools. Online gambling is illegal for US citizens, but the laws are seen as unenforceable. A University of Pennsylvania study found 2.9 million young people gambled at least once a week with cards, and 580,000 aged 14 to 22 gambled weekly on the net.

> ## There are 40 million online gamblers around the world. That number is predicted to quadruple by 2020

The number of high school and college students calling gambling helplines in America has doubled in the past two years. Ed Looney, who runs a helpline for the New Jersey Council on Compulsive Gambling, blames Internet poker. 'I have been in this field for 30 years and I've never seen anything as crazy as this,' says the reformed gambling addict. 'It's much like when crack cocaine came out in America in the Eighties. Internet gambling is something right now that you almost can't stop.'

Two years ago, Paul, a 17-year-old from New Jersey, stole his father's American Express card to play online poker. Within a few weeks it was $10,000 into the red. He hoped to win it back before his father found out, but was forced to confess when the bill arrived: his father had to pay up. Paul says the lure of the 24-hour online poker rooms was irresistible: 'There was no real age verification or proof of anything needed to play.'

Research by Professor Jeff Derevensky of McGill University's International Centre for Youth Gambling in Montreal found that teenage gamblers were almost three times as likely as adults to become addicted: 'Adolescents tend to be impulsive and think of themselves as risk-takers. The adrenalin rush is there whether they are winning or losing.'

Phil, a 21-year-old student from Manchester, says he started playing, legally, at 19. He lost £5,000 in three months. 'Internet gambling is vicious. My rent, my student loan, my overdrafts, whatever money I could get hold of went into [Internet gambling]. I borrowed £2,000 off my ex-girlfriend and used that just to gamble.'

Many sites abide by a strict code of practice, but an industry source said there were 'dozens of rogue outfits' based in places such as the Caribbean and the Far East. The gambling minister, Richard Caborn, agrees the industry remains the 'wild West' of gambling – near-impossible to police, at least until the Gambling Act comes fully into force next year.

In the meantime, says Caborn, underage players remain a matter of genuine concern. 'We're nowhere near even applying what is in the act, let alone dealing with the areas [that have been] pointed up. But the establishment of [new industry regulator] the Gambling Commission will change that and we will be taking tough action with companies which fail in their responsibilities in the very near future.'

12 March 2006

© *Guardian Newspapers Limited 2006*

Mobile gambling boom time ahead

Punters set to bet $23bn via their handsets...

By Will Sturgeon

The worldwide explosion in gambling, both online and offline, is set to see a further surge as the number of people gambling via their mobile phones looks ready to increase dramatically over the next five years.

The popularity of Internet sports betting has grown prolifically over the past five years and the recent boom in online casino gaming has added further fervour to the global gambling phenomenon.

As consumers grow accustomed to being able to gamble any time, any place, anywhere, it seems mobile phones are also set to become an increasingly important tool in the gambler's arsenal.

Juniper Research expects bets placed over mobile phone applications to rise from just under $2bn currently to in excess of $23bn by 2011

Juniper Research expects bets placed over mobile phone applications to rise from just under $2bn currently to in excess of $23bn by 2011, according to a forecast released today.

Lotteries are going to be the primary driver, as more users are turned on to low stakes gaming on their mobile phones. Juniper predicts mobile lotteries will account for 41 per cent of mobile gambling expenditure within five years.

The growth in 3G subscriptions as well as the introduction of increasingly sophisticated handsets with greater rich media capabilities will also make casino games a more attractive handheld offering, Juniper predicts.

But that won't be good news for everybody, especially those opposed to a 24/7 culture of gambling in the UK and the problems it creates, such as debt and related issues among gambling addicts.

Andrew Poole, a spokesman for charity GamCare, which works to help problem gamblers, told silicon.com he believes gambling in the UK is already 24/7 thanks to the Internet, though he admitted it could be more problematic if gamblers are even able to gamble while they are out and about, away from their computers.

Although Poole said take-up for text versions of the National Lottery has been low, instant win games such as casino games 'are a harder form of gambling and are more addictive in their nature'.

As such, he said it is important that as operators rush to create and meet demand for mobile gambling they also include responsible measures and adhere to codes of practice, such as limits on deposits or time which players can play for, to reduce the threat of problem gambling.
31 May 2006

⇨ The above information originally appeared on the silicon.com website and is reprinted with kind permission. For more information on this and other topics, please visit the silicon.com website at www.silicon.com

The problem with gambling

The coming of the UK's first supercasino and the increase in online gambling mean more people are gambling. And more people are becoming addicted to gambling...

Play your cards right

Gambling in this country has never been easier. Prior to the 2005 Gambling Act, when people wanted to gamble in UK casinos they had to take out a membership then wait 24 hours before making their first bet. Now anyone over 18 can walk into a casino and immediately start gambling.

Gambling is big business and the economic benefits – job creation, revenue in government coffers – are huge. But some people pay a big price

Around one million people regularly bet online, punters are no longer taxed and Britain's first supercasino is on its way. Not surprising then that, according to government research, £53billion was spent on non-online gambling in 2005.

All this is betting heaven for those who like the occasional flutter. But it's hell for those who become gambling addicts. The Salvation Army claims there are 370,000 problem gamblers in this country.

Women in particular seem to be becoming more susceptible to addiction. Gambling charity GamCare has revealed that two per cent of those seeking counselling were female in 2000. In the second half of 2005, that figure had risen to 18 per cent.

Faith Freestone, a therapist at the Gordon House Association – a residential centre that helps addicted gamblers – says, 'Traditionally, most

By James Lamb

women wouldn't be seen dead inside a bookmaker's. But we are finding more and more are happy to sit for hour after hour gambling online.'

Help at hand

But what is addiction? Gamblers Anonymous has a 20-point test to define an addict. Seven or more 'yes' answers to these questions define someone as a compulsive gambler.

The questions are similar to those asked of anyone with a possible addiction to alcohol or drugs. Essentially, does the habit adversely affect the person's lifestyle and the lifestyle of those around them? One former resident at Gordon House estimates she gambled £300,000 on roulette, though not all addiction has such extreme results.

If people realise they need help then they can contact organisations such as Gamblers Anonymous or GamCare. But it is important the addict makes that decision. That is the first step to recovery.

In an attempt to nip addiction in the bud, the government is looking to educate gamblers (while, of course, increasing their opportunities to gamble). The 2005 Gambling Act comes into force in September 2007 – it includes the guideline that operators must promote 'socially responsible gambling'.

Big stakes in the States

In the States, legal gambling (not including online gambling) raises revenues of $135.9 billion, of which $35.5 million is spent on educating and treating problem gamblers. The US example suggests profit wins out over social responsibility.

Gambling is big business and the economic benefits – job creation, revenue in government coffers – are huge. But some people pay a big price.

⇨ The above information is reprinted with kind permission from virgin.net. For more information, please visit their website at www.virgin.net

© virgin.net

Information on gambling

Information from the Mental Health Foundation

Introduction

The *Chambers Dictionary* defines gambling as:

1. Making a bet.
2. Playing a game of chance.
3. Taking a risk.

Most of us gamble once in a while e.g. by playing bingo, buying a lottery ticket or taking part in a raffle. And it's becoming increasingly easy to gamble, with the development of telephone/Internet gambling services and the opening of supercasinos in Britain.

It's becoming increasingly easy to gamble, with the development of telephone/Internet services and the opening of supercasinos

---

Why do we gamble?

People gamble for a whole range of reasons including:

- the buzz, the excitement, and the high adrenalin release
- the competitive element – trying to beat other players, the bookie, or the dealer
- the thrill of risk taking, of placing large bets
- to solve financial problems
- a way of escaping from stress or worries.

Sensible gambling

Some people say that there is no such thing as safe gambling. Others argue that gambling is like drinking alcohol – it's safe to do as long as you follow some sensible rules.

- Keep away from high-risk forms of gambling where you can lose large sums of money very quickly.
- Limit the amount of time you gamble. This will give you time to do other, more important things with your life.
- Limit the amount you spend to the amount you can afford to lose. When you have spent this much, walk away.
- Quit while you are ahead. If you continue, you are likely to lose because the odds are always stacked against you. Otherwise, how would the bookies and the casinos make their money?

When gambling becomes a problem

For most of us, gambling is a harmless activity. But, for some people, gambling is a way of life, an addiction that can wreck their lives.

You may be a compulsive gambler if:

- You spend more money on gambling than you can afford. If you continue to gamble, you could get into serious debt. You could also lose your home and your possessions.
- You spend so much time gambling that you neglect other important areas of your life, like your family or your work. You could lose your job or end up divorced or separated from your partner and children.
- Your feelings and behaviour change. For example, you may become depressed when you lose or overexcited when you win.

And, in serious cases, you may feel that you are only really alive when you gamble.

- It leads you to inappropriate or even criminal behaviour. For example, you may lie to family and friends about your gambling activities or you may steal to fund your gambling habit.

Questions to ask yourself

If you think you may have a gambling problem but are not sure, ask yourself:

- Is gambling making me unhappy at work or at home?
- Is gambling making it hard to sleep at night or concentrate during the day?
- Am I lying to other people and myself about how much I gamble?
- Am I gambling to get away from problems or worries?
- Am I gambling to get money – so that I can pay off debts or solve financial problems?
- Am I borrowing money or selling possessions so that I can gamble?
- If I have just won or just lost, do I feel I need to gamble just a little bit more?

If you answered yes to any of these questions, then you may have a gambling problem.

What causes compulsive gambling?

All compulsive behaviours have social, psychological and biological origins. Gambling brings us into contact with others even if through virtual means. This can provide a sense of community – however damaging the associated behaviours. Social meaning and acceptance by others are important to us all and for the compulsive gambler these can be found in virtual gaming rooms, real casinos, bookmakers and so on.

Gambling alters how we feel psychologically as well as socially. It allows us to escape our normal lives and the everyday struggles we experience

Gambling also alters how we feel psychologically as well as socially. It allows us to escape our normal lives and the everyday struggles we experience. During a period of gambling our mind is occupied by the odds, the bet, the race, the actions of other gamers, the run of the cards and so on. It can be all consuming and therefore provides an engaging, exciting escape from ordinary life.

At the biological level compulsive behaviours can have a direct effect on the brain's dopamine reward system. This system regulates our responses to natural rewards like food, sex and social interaction. Repeated compulsive behaviours can act on this system with a power and persistence that changes its cells both chemically and structurally. This in turn can have an overwhelming effect on our wellbeing. Thus, people may no longer respond normally to rewards such as food, sex and social interaction, needing instead to depend on gambling for their sense of reward.

Compulsive gambling can therefore develop through the social meaning and psychological relief that it offers. This is further compounded by the chemical changes in our brain that accompany these experiences. It is in fact artificial to separate these factors since they all occur simultaneously for the compulsive gambler. Social meaning, psychological relief and a fired dopamine reward system can be a difficult combination of experiences for the most hardy of individuals to resist.

Helping yourself

If you feel that you have lost control of your gambling, there are some things you can do to help yourself:
⇨ Admitting you have a problem is the first and most important step.
⇨ Find someone you can trust to talk to about your problem. It could be a friend, a relative or a specialist advisor.
⇨ Avoid locations and situations where you may be tempted to gamble.
⇨ Take control of how you spend your money, so that you don't waste it on gambling.
⇨ If you can't do this by yourself, you may need to ask someone else to help you do this.
⇨ Take one day at a time. Don't expect everything to improve straight away.

Living with someone who gambles

Living with someone who gambles can be just as difficult as living with someone with any other kind of addiction. It can be very stressful and it can lead to the breakdown of your relationship.

If you are not sure whether you are living with someone who has a gambling problem, ask yourself:
⇨ Do they promise time and time again to stop gambling but carry on anyway?
⇨ Do they disappear for long periods of time without telling you where they were?
⇨ Do they spend large sums of money without being able to account for it?
⇨ Do you hide money to stop them spending it?
⇨ Do they lie to cover up or deny their gambling?

If you answered yes to most of these questions, then they may have a gambling problem.

How to help someone who gambles

It is important to remember you are not the only person in this situation and there are lots of people who can help.

Things you can do:
⇨ Talk it through with the other person and, if necessary, get professional help.

⇨ Be firm and constructive. You need to make sure the other person actually faces the problem but also has some ideas of how to move things forward.
⇨ Do not condemn them or try to make them feel bad about themselves. Just telling them to 'snap out of it' may not help and could actually make it worse.
⇨ Be realistic. Compulsive gambling is an addiction, so it will take them time to overcome it. Some days will be better than others.
⇨ Do not trust them with money until they have overcome the addiction.

⇨ Reproduced from the Mental Health Foundation website with their permission. For the most up-to-date information on this and other issues, please visit www.mentalhealth.org.uk

© *Mental Health Foundation*

Gambling 'as addictive as crack cocaine'

Gambling can be as dangerous and addictive as taking drugs, experts said yesterday.

A scientist specialising in addiction warned there is little biological difference between what goes on in the heads of compulsive gamblers and crack addicts.

Dr Eric Nestler accused the Government of feeding the problem by relaxing gambling laws.

He said 'Gambling is a government-subsidised addiction.

'Gambling is a government-subsidised addiction'

'We need to be made more aware of the potential risks and we need to remove subsidies for addictive behaviours – tobacco, gambling, state lotteries – it is absurd.'

The Texan psychiatrist also criticised politicians for not doing more to prevent teenagers becoming hooked on slot machines, adding: 'They are one of the most addictive forms of gambling available.'

Dr Nestler's research has shown gamblers' brains react to risk in much the same way as a drug addict's does to narcotics.

He told the magazine *New Scientist*: 'Take a person with sex addiction or a pathological gambler, their brains all show abnormal responses – the same reactions to drugs.'

Studies show gamblers experience cravings triggered by images of their favourite games comparable to the response of drug addicts.

British research shows gamblers have withdrawal symptoms like those experienced by addicts denied drugs. Professor Mark Griffiths, of Nottingham Trent University, found gamblers who cannot feed their habit suffer from moodiness, irritability, nausea, stomach cramps and sweats.

By Fiona MacRae, Science Reporter

'These are real effects,' he said. 'Gamblers have withdrawal symptoms like drug addicts.'

The psychologist, who has spent 20 years studying the minds of gamblers, believes many of the key features of crack, heroin, alcohol and nicotine addiction apply to gambling.

The addiction dominates the person's mind, leading to cravings and a total preoccupation with the habit.

They also build up a tolerance to their habit, leading to a need to increase their 'fix' over time.

The heart rate of gamblers goes up when they play slot machines, creating a rush similar to a drugs high.

In new or less experienced players, the rate remains high for the duration of play, but in regular gamblers the rise is only transient.

So, to maintain the effect, they have to gamble faster and longer and take greater risks.

Professor Jim Orford, an addiction expert from Birmingham University, believe addictions such as gambling threaten us all. He said: 'Almost any of us can become behavioural addicts, given the right exposure, the right timing and so on.'

British research shows gamblers have withdrawal symptoms like those experienced by addicts denied drugs

Dr Peter Whybrow, a Californian psychiatrist, said: 'We have created a fabulous new environment with lots of wonderful opportunities.

'If politicians understood how the brain works, they would not be building the society they are doing.'

⇨ This article first appeared in the *Daily Mail*, 24 August 2006.

© 2006 Associated Newspapers Ltd

Doctors fear boom in gambling addiction

Information from the Press Association

Supercasinos and Internet gambling could lead to a huge rise in the number of addicts, doctors said today.

Calling for more research into treatments and prevention on the NHS, doctors attending the

British Medical Association's annual conference said addicts descended into a 'nightmare world'.

Dr David Sinclair, from Fife, proposed a motion calling for the BMA Board of Science to examine the issue more closely.

He said gambling 'starts off as safe and fun' but there was a 'dark, dark side of gambling'.

Internet gambling and supercasinos 'are making us think about treatment options', he added.

'We know gambling addiction rises with increasing availability but we don't know about treatment.'

Dr Sinclair said gambling was considered the 'Cinderella addiction' behind drugs and alcohol.

The industry is now worth £40 billion a year, but the Government has plans for a supercasino and several smaller ones.

Dr Jan Wise, a GP from London, spoke in favour of the motion, which was passed by doctors at the Annual Representatives' Meeting.

He said research showed that 5% of 12- to 15-year-olds show signs of addiction while 75% of the same age group say they have played slot machines.

More than a third (40%) say they have also played the National Lottery.

Dr Wise said between 275,000 and 350,000 adults in the UK could be defined as gambling addicts. He said it was difficult for an independent observer to tell somebody who enjoys gambling at which point it becomes an addiction.

It could be as simple as being half an hour late back from a lunch break 'because you are at the bookies' or could relate to how much was being spent.

He added: 'An addict will be spending much more than they think they are.

'We are asking the Board of Science to look into treatment and to compare our approach with other countries.

'The relaxation of the gambling laws means it's only going to become more and more of an issue.

'Treatment is not with drugs, there's no pill.'

'In some people the descent is quite often destitution through gambling and then drugs and alcohol to cope with that.'

Research showed that 5% of 12- to 15-year-olds show signs of addiction while 75% of the same age group say they have played slot machines

---

He said some therapies had been shown to work such as showing people how to seek thrills elsewhere.

He added: 'We need to get them to examine what it is that's missing in their lives that gets them to do this.

'Treating gambling addiction is not heart surgery.'

28 June 2006

© *Press Association*

One in 10 Scottish children is gambling addict

⇨ *Survey of 2,000 Scots pupils finds 9.7% have a gambling problem*

⇨ *Campaigners demand age restrictions on slot machines*

⇨ *Average Scot spends three times as much on gambling as four years ago*

'Gambling in children is not obvious, like smoking, drinking or physical abuse, but it is there. Advice on gambling needs to be part of the school curriculum' – Sousana Mesimeri, deputy project leader RCA Trust.

By Louise Gray, Scottish Political Correspondent

Almost one in ten Scottish children is a problem gambler, with some as young as 11 skipping school to feed fruit machines, the first extensive study into the problem has revealed.

The survey of more than 2,000 pupils from 12 schools across west central Scotland found nine per cent were exhibiting behaviour that could lead to a fully fledged gambling addiction later on in life. In England and Wales the figure is six per cent.

A further 15 per cent of Scottish children are deemed to be at risk of developing a gambling habit.

Researchers believe there is a direct link between problem gambling in childhood and a fully fledged adult addiction which has reached record levels in Scotland.

The average Scottish adult now spends almost £1,900 a year on games of chance – three times as much as four years ago. Gamblers Anonymous has reported a 200 per cent rise in the number of addicts attending its Edinburgh meetings alone.

Campaigners said the new research into children's gambling habits showed the urgent need for new age restrictions to be introduced on all slot machines.

The team from Glasgow Caledonian University questioned the children about their gambling habits, including whether they had missed school to gamble, if they felt it difficult to stop gambling, if they became tense and irritable if asked to stop, or if they had experienced problems with their family because of the habit.

The study revealed that 9.7 per cent of secondary school pupils aged 13 or 14 had a problem with their gambling; as did 8.6 per cent of students aged 15 or 16.

Of the smaller number of primary school pupils aged 11 or 12 interviewed, 5.9 per cent had a problem, with almost half of those skipping school to gamble.

The results also found that boys are 3.5 times more likely to be problem gamblers than girls.

Crawford Moodie, a psychologist at Glasgow Caledonian and author of the study, was prompted to look into the issue because of the 'dearth of information' about youth gambling in Scotland. He found a higher number of underage problem gamblers than in England and Wales, and certainly than the rest of Europe, where gambling on fruit machines is illegal for under-16s in most countries.

The study found fruit machines are the most popular form of gambling. Under-16s in Scotland are only allowed legally to gamble on 'Category D' fruit machines that pay out a £5 jackpot for 10p stakes.

However, Mr Moodie said these machines are difficult to tell from higher category machines, making it easy for children to bet more serious money.

Also, the machines teach children to become addicted to the adrenalin and rewards from gambling.

Children with gambling problems spent an average of £4.35 a week on the habit, almost a fifth of their weekly income and a large amount for a child. They were also more likely to smoke and drink.

Next year the Gambling Act will see the setting up of 17 new casinos in Britain including a supercasino. The government claims children will be better protected, but Mr Moodie is expecting the problem to get worse.

'I would expect with the global expansion of legalised gambling and the increase in accessibility and availability, and the technical advances in gambling through the Internet, to see an increase in youth gambling,' he said.

Irene McLaughlin, the Scottish co-ordinator of the counselling service GamCare, said the organisation has seen a massive increase in recent years, with fears that as many as 100,000 Scots are secretly battling some form of betting problem.

She said: 'Fruit machines are seen as not problematic but it is dangerous because it is a learned behaviour and if there is an award system that learned behaviour is reinforced.'

Ms McLaughlin called for a rise in the age limit on fruit machines in Scotland and education on the dangers of gambling.

The Department of Culture, Media and Sport said the act will protect children by increasing the powers of the regulatory body, the Gambling Commission, to punish any premises allowing children to gamble and restricting the areas where slot machines are allowed.

Nine per cent of Scottish schoolchildren surveyed were exhibiting behaviour that could lead to a fully fledged gambling addiction later on in life. In England and Wales the figure is six per cent

---

However, Fergus Ewing, SNP MSP for Inverness East, Nairn and Lochaber, said the new casinos, with their glamour and accessibility, will make it worse for children. 'Many individual lives will be ruined. The children of Britain are going to be exposed to a risk of gambling addiction on a scale hitherto unknown.'

Losing the habit

Like most gamblers, John kept believing he would win. But at the age of just 15, he was losing £100 a week at the local arcade. John was the first child to be treated for a gambling problem at the RCA Trust, a counselling service in Renfrewshire.

The schoolboy was referred by social workers after being arrested for trying to steal an elderly woman's purse. Although he was from a comfortable home and doing well at school, it soon emerged he had a gambling problem.

The habit started innocently enough on the 'puggies' – slot machines – while skipping school. However, John soon became addicted to the thrill of betting and was spending £60 a week from a part-time job as well as pocket money and the proceeds of theft.

RCA forced John to keep a diary to make him realise how much he was spending, helped him to control the need for an impulsive thrill and gave him money-management courses.

Sousana Mesimeri, deputy project leader for young people's services at the trust, said if a child's problem gambling was not addressed it could become worse in adulthood.

'Gambling in children is not obvious, like smoking, drinking or physical abuse, but it is there,' she said. 'Advice on gambling needs to be part of the school curriculum.'
⇨ John is not the boy's real name.
2 August 2006
© Scotsman Publications Ltd

Story of a teenage problem gambler

Information from the Salvation Army

My name is Pete. I am now 23 years old and live and work in South London. I can't remember exactly when I started gambling but it started to be something I specifically remember enjoying when I was about 12 or 13. This was playing on fruit machines at the arcades when we used to go on holiday to Weymouth in Dorset. Even at this stage, the continuous buzz of the fruit machine got me hooked and I often ended up spending most or all of my holiday pocket money.

When I was 14, I was allowed out of my school grounds at lunch times and would often go to the local bowling alley where there were 5p fruit machines and would spend my lunch money plus any more I could get my hands on. At this stage sometimes I would get lucky and win a jackpot but for some reason I would always end up putting it back in so I guess even by this stage I was properly addicted.

As I got older and at 16 went to college I started to go into bookmakers' and play on the higher value machines as well as starting to gamble on the horses and the greyhounds. After 6 months of college I had to drop out as I had not attended college enough as I had been gambling. This was all very secretive because I didn't want people to know how much or how often I gambled because inevitably the question would come as to where the finance came from. Of course the answer is that it was stolen, from my family, from my friends and from my workplace. I'm deeply ashamed of this and am still trying to pay some of these debts back now.

I finally hit rock bottom when I spent over £1,000 in 3 days on gambling and was found out by my family. This was when I had to face up to it, and despite a lot of hurt I live my life normally now. I believe that I have been able to turn away from gambling for many reasons including the support I have received but I believe a lot is down to the fact that I am an adult now and am able to understand the consequences of my actions better.

The addiction still affects me now in that I am still paying off debts due to gambling and because I am still tempted to gamble now. As a child, playing on fruit machines caused me to steal, caused me to truant and the effects of these things have had a major impact on my life.

⇨ The above information is taken from a meeting with Peers in the House of Lords on 8 February 2005 and is reprinted with kind permission from the Salvation Army, 101 Newington Causeway, SE1 6BN. Visit www.salvationarmy.org.uk for more information.
© Salvation Army

More women seeking help over gambling addiction

An increasing number of women are seeking help over an addiction to gambling.

Advice charity GamCare said growing numbers of its counselling clients and helpline callers were female while a quarter of addicts using its website forum were now women.

The charity said in a report given to the BBC that the issue had only recently begun to receive the attention it needed.

According to the report, women represented 9% of counselling clients and 18% of helpline callers in the second half of 2005.

Advice charity GamCare said growing numbers of its counselling clients and helpline callers were female while a quarter of addicts using its website forum were now women

---

This compares with figures showing that women made up just 2% of clients in 2000.

The total number of people approaching the charity for counselling rose 41.3% from 2004 to 6,563 in 2005, the report added.

A spokesperson for GamCare told the BBC that women were still under-represented among clients coming forward for addiction counselling.

'Why women are not being seen in greater numbers is complex. Stigma and shame are likely to be strong factors,' the charity said.

The report came as local councils across the country waited to hear whether they had made the shortlist of areas to host the UK's first Las Vegas-style supercasino.

Only one of the 27 local councils that applied will be allowed to host the giant regional gambling venue with 1,250 unlimited jackpot slot machines.

The independent body set up to recommend to Culture Secretary Tessa Jowell which it should be is expected to draw up a shortlist tomorrow.

The Casino Advisory Panel has spent the last few weeks examining the detailed bids that had to be submitted by the end of March.

It is due to deliver its final decision to Ms Jowell by the end of the year but reports suggested as many as 12 on the shortlist.

Among the favourites are the Millennium Dome, Blackpool, Glasgow and Manchester.

The councils that submitted bids for a supercasino were: Blackpool, Brent, Cardiff, Chesterfield, Coventry, Dartford, Dudley, Glasgow, Great Yarmouth, Greenwich, Havering, Hull, Ipswich, Leeds, Manchester, Middlesbrough, Midlothian, Newcastle, Newport, Sheffield, Solihull, Southampton, Southend-on-Sea, Sunderland, Thurrock, Wakefield and West Dunbartonshire.

Social and regeneration impacts will be considered by the panel.

Before last year's General Election, Ms Jowell struck a deal with the Tories to save the Gambling Bill by agreeing to scale down plans for eight regional casinos to just one.

Some MPs have called for more, claiming it would be impossible to measure the impact of the new-style casinos if they were limited to only one area.

But Labour's John Grogan said the cap should not be lifted.

'I am sceptical about whether we should have any unlimited stakes and unlimited prizes. They are extremely addictive,' he told BBC2's *Newsnight*.

'In Britain we have the lowest problem gambling rates in the OECD, less than one in a hundred gamblers has a problem.

'In Australia, where these machines are prevalent, you have three or four.'

He added: 'When you look at places like Atlantic City, yes you've got some jobs in the supercasino but over 20 years there has been a chilling effect on the area around.

'Many businesses, hotels and smaller gambling businesses have gone out of business, so we want to be very cautious about this.

'Let's test it in one area and see what happens, but let's not let rip.'

23 May 2006

© *Press Association*

Signs and interventions for a gambling dependency

Information from GamCare

Gambling dependency

A gambling dependency is difficult to spot. It has been called the 'hidden addiction' because:

⇨ There are no physical symptoms as there are with drug abuse or alcoholism;

⇨ Gamblers frequently do not believe they have 'a problem' or wish to hide it;

⇨ Gamblers are exceedingly plausible and become adept at concocting believable stories to mask the truth;

⇨ Money shortages and debts can be explained away with ease;

⇨ With young people, gambling may be only one of several excessive behaviours.

There are, however, a number of signs and symptoms which, when taken together, indicate that gambling may be the problem. The more probable signs are listed in this article.

Many of these signs can also be applied to other excessive behaviours, so caution must be exercised before deciding that gambling is the problem.

Signs and symptoms

1. Clear indications

⇨ Request for help from gambler.

⇨ Admission by gambler that he or she spends too much money on gambling.

⇨ Gambler saying that they spend too much time gambling and cannot keep away.

⇨ Gambling seen as legitimate means of making money.

⇨ Persuading friends to gamble against their will.

⇨ Gambling alone for long periods.

⇨ Frequenting amusement arcades, betting shops, horse and dog tracks, or casinos several times a week.

⇨ Spending excessive time playing on Internet gambling sites.

⇨ Spending more than they can afford on the Lottery.

⇨ Committing crime to fund gambling or pay off gambling debts.

⇨ Persistent reports that a person has been seen gambling and in the informer's view has a problem.

⇨ Frequently in possession of fruit machine tokens, betting slips, scratchcards, etc.

2. Probable indications

⇨ Money difficulties and debts that are cleared and then reappear.

⇨ Unrealistic suggestions to pay off debts.

⇨ Criminal offences of fraud, embezzlement, and persistent theft of cash.

⇨ No apparent interests, pastimes or leisure pursuits.

⇨ High degree of knowledge about gambling.

⇨ Blind optimism, looks at short-term prospects and is only concerned with the 'here and now'.

⇨ Creates rows at home as an excuse to go out.

⇨ Pockets/purse full of coins.

⇨ Strenuous denial when challenged that gambling is a problem.

3. Possible indications

⇨ Parent(s) had gambling problem or gambled frequently.

⇨ Need to show off skills or achieve group status.

⇨ Poor school/work results compared to ability level.

⇨ Truancy, college or work absenteeism.

⇨ Dinner money misused – coming home persistently very hungry.

⇨ Mood swings, irritability, restlessness.

⇨ Very low, depressed, preoccupied, withdrawn.

⇨ Lying to cover tracks or disguise money shortages.

⇨ Lack of, or half-hearted interest in children, other family members or friends.

⇨ Isolated, lonely, and with no time at all for friends.

⇨ Suicide attempt(s).

⇨ Working in a job that allows time to slip away and gamble.

- ⇨ Lack of instant accountability in a job.
- ⇨ Always has a ready excuse as to why short of money.
- ⇨ Workaholic attitude, seems to have drive and energy.
- ⇨ Saleable and valuable items go missing from home.
- ⇨ Very competitive, always likes to win, bad loser.

Interventions for a gambling dependency

Understand the issues
Gain what knowledge you can about the issues of gambling – both positive and negative.

Gambling dependency has been called the 'hidden addiction' because there are no physical symptoms as there are with drug abuse or alcoholism

---

Structure change
Adapt a method of changing behaviour you have used with other problems (such as alcohol or drug dependency), or develop one that is realistic and attainable.

Understanding their motivation
Escaping from an unhappy life, missing work or studies to gamble.

Money as a tool
Even after great losses, the impulsive need to continue gambling as soon as possible in an attempt to win back what's gone.

Total lack of interest
No interest in family and friends, borrows or steals to support their gambling habit.

Driven by despair
Creates arguments, feelings of frustration and disappointment, gambling becomes their release. Depressed or even suicidal over gambling.

Manage finances
Debt counselling will almost certainly be needed, and the control and accountability of all money may be required. If mutually agreed, it can help a gambler initially if a trusted friend/family member holds the gambler's finances until their confidence in managing money is restored.

GamCare helpline: 0845 6000 133

⇨ The above information is reprinted with kind permission from GamCare, the National Association for Gambling Care. Visit www.gamcare.org.uk for more.

© GamCare

Gambling debt

If you can't call it a day before your luck turns, read on . . .

Inside tip

- ⇨ People gamble on almost any kind of outcome, from football to horse and greyhound racing, even the chances of Steps headlining next year's Ozzfest (2 gazillion to 1).
- ⇨ Lottery scratchcards and slot machines are a big draw among 18- to 24-year-olds, though online casinos are proving very popular.
- ⇨ The appeal is in thinking you might win, though ultimately it's the gambling industry that cleans up. Check out the odds:
  - ↳ Winning eight quid on a fruit machine: 600 to 1
  - ↳ Fifty thou' scratchcard jackpot: 2.57million to 1
  - ↳ Lottery jackpot: 14.5 million to 1
  - ↳ Football pools win: 7.5 million to 1.

Losing streak

- ⇨ Gambling raises blood pressure, heart rate and adrenalin levels – creating a buzz that can get some people coming back for more.
- ⇨ This is known as 'compulsive' gambling – a progressive mental disorder that leaves sufferers unable to resist the impulse to gamble – often as a means of escaping from problems such as stress, anxiety or depression.
- ⇨ People with gambling dependency difficulties believe that money will solve their problems – a belief that is reinforced as the debts begin to mount.
- ⇨ The disruption to their lives isn't just financial, and can affect relationships and careers.

All bets off?

Can you resist a flutter? Ask yourself these searching questions:
- ⇨ Have you ever skipped college/work due to gambling?
- ⇨ Does the amount you spend on gambling tend to grow?
- ⇨ Are you touchy about people asking after your habit?
- ⇨ Are you prone to mood swings, and turn to gambling as a means of changing the way you feel?
- ⇨ Do you gamble after arguments or if you're feeling hassled?
- ⇨ After losing, do you feel the need to gamble again in the hope of reclaiming your money?
- ⇨ Do you boast about a win, and lie to cover up losing?

⇨ The above information is reprinted with kind permission from TheSite.org. Visit www.thesite.org for more information.

© TheSite.org

Gamblers Anonymous and GamAnon

Information from Gamblers Anonymous

Gamblers Anonymous

Main purpose

To help compulsive gamblers to overcome their gambling problem.

Who can seek help/join?

For men and women, of any age, who want to do something about their gambling problem and help other compulsive gamblers to do the same.

Helplines

The helplines operate 24 hours a day, every day. They offer an opportunity to talk about personal gambling problems and to learn the way in which GA can help to stop compulsive gambling.

The helplines give information about the nearest Gamblers Anonymous group, and can arrange to send literature for individuals or helping agencies.

Meetings

Held in most major towns and cities in England, Ireland, Scotland and Wales. The fellowship is not religious, and has no professional guidance or support.

The only requirement for membership is a desire to stop gambling.

Members are encouraged to persist in spite of setbacks. At their meetings, members are helped towards a programme of recovery through practical advice which includes weekly budgeting to repay debts.

GamAnon

Main purpose

To offer support to families and friends of gamblers.

Who can seek help/join?

Families and friends of compulsive gamblers regardless of whether the gambler attends GA.

Helplines

The helplines operate 24 hours a day, every day. They offer an opportunity for the family and friends of a compulsive gambler to talk over their difficulties.

The helplines provide information about the nearest GamAnon group where mutual support and encouragement is available to the families and friends of compulsive gamblers.

Meetings

GamAnon meetings are usually on the same nights as GA meetings but are in separate rooms. The two fellowships do not share experiences or information about each other.

Gamblers Anonymous is for men and women, of any age, who want to do something about their gambling problem and help other compulsive gamblers to do the same

---

GamAnon provides support and encouragement for the families and friends of compulsive gamblers, and helps them to understand the problem and to help in overcoming it.

They are welcome even if the gambler does not cooperate.

Funding

These are both voluntary organisations and voluntary self-financing is part of the recovery programme to cover the cost of group meetings, fellowship literature, and the helplines. They refuse outside contributions.

Direct approach or by referral?

Anyone can ring the helplines, whether to seek help for themselves or to obtain information on how gamblers and their families can be helped.

Talks

There are members of Gamblers Anonymous and GamAnon in most regions willing to talk at seminars or other gatherings about their experiences to help encourage compulsive gamblers seek the assistance of Gamblers Anonymous. Please use the helpline if more detailed information is needed.

Prison Liaison and Public Relations

There are appointed members responsible for Prison Liaison and Public Relations in most regions.

Shared address

PO Box 5382, London W1A 6SA
info@gamblersanonymous.org.uk
contactus@gamanon.org.uk
www.gamblersanonymous.org.uk
www.gamanon.org.uk
Shared helpline: 020 7384 3040

Help with the diagnosis of compulsive gambling

The following is intended to assist in the diagnosis of compulsive gambling and is based on research and observation by professionals over many years.

Some popular descriptions that indicate the presence of compulsive gambling. (Any ONE would apply):

⇨ Individuals with a progressive failure to resist impulses to gambling. Gambling behaviour that compromises, disrupts, or damages personal, family or vocational pursuits.

⇨ Concern on the part of the gambler's family about the amount of time and money spent gambling, which is considered to be excessive.

⇨ An overpowering urge to gamble so that the individual may be intermittently or continuously preoccupied with thought of gambling. Usually associated with tension that is found to be relieved by further gambling.

⇨ Individual who fails to resist the impulse or temptation to gamble, even though he/she has tried to do so. Experiences increasing tension before gambling and is preoccupied with gambling when trying to work or do other things. Has feelings of pleasure, justification, or release at the time of gambling.

In addition to the above, at least THREE of the following would usually also be true:

⇨ Committed a crime.

⇨ Defaulted on debts or other financial responsibilities.

⇨ Disrupted relationship with spouse or family.

⇨ Borrowing money at excessive interest rates.

⇨ Unable to account for loss of money or to produce evidence of winning money, if this is claimed.

⇨ Loss of work due to absenteeism.

⇨ Necessity for another person to provide money to relieve a desperate situation.

Associated features. Any of which may help confirm diagnosis, but which cannot be considered in isolation from the symptoms above.

In the gambling context:

⇨ The gambling is chronic but waxes and wanes.

⇨ Dreams of the 'Big Win' and fantasises that this week's win will overcome last week's losses.

⇨ Unwilling to think about stopping gambling.

⇨ The belief that life without gambling is impossible.

⇨ The belief that gambling can be controlled by willpower.

Other characteristics and traits:

⇨ Over-confident, somewhat abrasive, very energetic. Usual response to family or friends: 'Don't worry about it!'

⇨ Signs of personal stress, anxiety and depression.

⇨ Neglecting responsibilities.

⇨ Wide mood swings.

⇨ Escapes to other excesses (alcohol, drugs, sleep).

⇨ Lack of interest in social activities.

⇨ Lack of physical childhood affection.

Most compulsive gamblers answer yes to at least seven of these questions:

1 Do you lose time from work due to gambling?

2 Is gambling making your home life unhappy?

3 Is gambling affecting your reputation?

4 Have you ever felt remorse after gambling?

5 Do you ever gamble to get money with which to pay debts or to otherwise solve financial difficulties?

6 Does gambling cause a decrease in your ambition or efficiency?

7 After losing, do you feel you must return as soon as possible and win back your losses?

8 After a win do you have a strong urge to return and win more?

9 Do you often gamble until your last pound is gone?

10 Do you ever borrow to finance your gambling?

11 Have you ever sold anything to finance gambling?

12 Are you reluctant to use gambling money for normal expenditures?

13 Does gambling make you careless of the welfare of your family?

14 Do you gamble longer than you planned?

15 Do you ever gamble to escape worry or trouble?

16 Have you ever committed, or considered committing, an illegal act to finance gambling?

17 Does gambling cause you to have difficulty in sleeping?

18 Do arguments, disappointments, or frustrations create an urge within you to gamble?

19 Do you have an urge to celebrate any good fortune by a few hours' gambling?

20 Have you ever considered self-destruction as a result of your gambling?

Questions for a young gambler to ask him/herself:

1 Do you stay away from school or work to gamble?

2 Do you gamble to escape from a boring and unhappy life?

3 When gambling and you run out of money do you feel lost and in despair, and need to gamble again as soon as possible?

4 Do you gamble until your last penny is gone, even the bus fare home or the cost of a cup of tea?

5 Have you lied, stolen or borrowed just to get money to gamble?

6 Are you reluctant to spend 'gambling money' on normal things?

7 Do you take any interest in your family?

8 Do you find it difficult to concentrate on your job or education?

9 Do arguments, frustrations, disappointments make you want to gamble?

10 Have you ever thought of suicide as a way of solving your problems?

⇨ The above information is reprinted with kind permission from Gamblers Anonymous. Visit www.gamblersanonymous.org.uk for more information.

© Gamblers Anonymous

Drug may curb pathological gambling

Information from the *American Journal of Psychiatry*

The impulse control disorder drug nalmefene, which has previously been shown to be effective for alcohol dependence, may also be effective for pathological gambling, according to a study.

The impulse control disorder drug nalmefene, which has previously been shown to be effective for alcohol dependence, may also be effective for pathological gambling, according to a study

'Pathological gambling is a disabling disorder experienced by approximately 1 per cent to 2 per cent of adults and for which there are few empirically validated treatments,' Dr Jon E. Grant, of the University of Minnesota Medical School, Minneapolis, and colleagues explain in the *American Journal of Psychiatry*.

'Pathological gambling is a disabling disorder experienced by approximately 1 per cent to 2 per cent of adults'

They assessed the value of nalmefene, a long-acting opioid antagonist, in 207 pathological gamblers randomised to nalmefene at 25 mg, 50 mg or 100 mg per day or inactive placebo. Twenty-four of the 51 patients in the placebo group and 49 of the 156 subject patients assigned to nalmefene completed the 16-week trial.

Fifty-nine per cent of the subjects in the 25-mg group were rated as 'much improved' or 'very much improved' at the last evaluation, compared with 34 per cent of those in the placebo group, Grant's team reports.

Although 48 per cent of those in the 50-mg group and 42 per cent of those in the 100-mg group were considered responders, the response rate was not significantly different from that seen in the placebo group.

Most adverse events were mild to moderate, and most occurred during the first week of treatment. The most common adverse events included nausea, dizziness and insomnia.

Approximately two-thirds of the patients did not complete the trial, which the researchers believe was primarily due to poor management of side effects. However, about half of the patients in pathologic gambling trials discontinue treatment, the researchers note.

10 March 2006

⇨ Information from the *American Journal of Psychiatry*. Visit http://ajp.psychiatryonline.org for more information.

Gambling by year

Money spent on gambling, by year.

£ millions at 2002/03 prices[1]

National Lottery (total)

Casinos[3]

Bingo clubs[3]

Lotteries (excluding National Lottery)[2]

1992/3 1993/4 1994/5 1995/6 1996/7 1997/8 1998/9 1999/00 2000/01 2001/02 2002/03

1. Adjusted to real terms using Retail Prices Index.
2. From 2002-03 includes Hotspot lotteries.
3. Great Britain only.

Sources: Department for Culture, Media and Sport: 020 7211 6121; Gaming Board for Great Britain: 020 7306 6253

⇨ Popular gambling activities in our society are: National Lottery and scratchcards, football pools, fruit/slot machines, bingo, betting on horse/dog racing, gambling in casinos, betting on sports events, private card games, raffles. Increasingly, opportunities to gamble are becoming available through new technology, e.g. Internet, WAP phones, interactive television. (page 1)

⇨ The majority of gaming machines (40.1%) are located in pubs. (page 3)

⇨ The estimated annual turnover of gambling activities in the UK is about £53 billion, according to 2005 figures from the National Audit Office. (page 4)

⇨ Tax calculations suggest that 78% of the British population gambled at some point during 2005. (page 6)

⇨ National Lottery players have helped to raise more than £18.6 billion for Good Causes to date. (page 9)

⇨ The first National Lottery draw took place on 19 November 1994. (page 10)

⇨ Fruit machines remain the most popular form of underage gambling for under 16s with over half of young people (54%) saying they have ever played on them and 49% in the past year. (page 11)

⇨ Boys are more likely than girls to be problem gamblers and prevalence of problem gambling rises with increasing disposable income. (page 13)

⇨ Research in the US has shown that six per cent of people living near supercasinos become gambling addicts. (page 14)

⇨ Gambling is becoming an increasingly mainstream pastime. Over a third of Britons bet on the Grand National, the country's single biggest gambling event. (page 16)

⇨ £5bn a year is wagered online with 93% of people with Internet access having gambled on the web. The average spend per week on gaming sites is between £10 and £20. (page 17)

⇨ A 2006 report predicted that the number of online gamblers in the UK will grow from 1.1m to 2.1m over the next four years. (page 19)

⇨ More than 14 million Europeans, or 14% of those online from home, visited a gambling and sweepstakes site in February 2005. (page 20)

⇨ GamCare states that in 2000 only two per cent of those seeking help for problem gambling were women, compared with nine per cent of those seeking counselling in 2006 and 18 per cent of calls received to the GamCare helpline. (page 21)

⇨ Research shows that by the time most compulsive gamblers seek help, they are hugely in debt and their family life is a shambles. About 80% seriously consider suicide, and up to 20% attempt or succeed in killing themselves. (page 23)

⇨ It is currently illegal to run poker and casino betting sites in Britain, but from January 2007 firms can apply to set up an infinite number under the Gambling Act 2005. (page 24)

⇨ There are 40 million online gamblers around the world. That number is predicted to quadruple by 2020. (page 25)

⇨ Juniper Research expects bets placed over mobile phone applications to rise from just under $2bn currently to in excess of $23bn by 2011, according to a forecast study released in May 2006. (page 26)

⇨ Some people say that there is no such thing as safe gambling. Others argue that gambling is like drinking alcohol – it's safe to do as long as you follow some sensible rules. (page 28)

⇨ A scientist specialising in addiction warned there is little biological difference between what goes on in the heads of compulsive gamblers and crack addicts. (page 30)

⇨ Research showed that 5% of 12- to 15-year-olds show signs of addiction while 75% of the same age group say they have played slot machines. (page 31)

⇨ Survey of 2,000 Scottish pupils finds 9.7% have a gambling problem. (page 32)

⇨ The odds of winning the National Lottery jackpot are 14.5 million to one. (page 36)

⇨ Gambling raises blood pressure, heart rate and adrenalin levels – creating a buzz that can get some people coming back for more. (page 36)

⇨ The impulse control disorder drug nalmefene, which has previously been shown to be effective for alcohol dependence, may also be effective for pathological gambling, according to a study published in the *American Journal of Psychiatry* in March 2006. (page 39)

GLOSSARY

Bingo
A numbers game where the winner has to be the first one to match random numbers printed on a card to those being called out.

Casino
A building where licensed gambling takes place. Popular casino games include roulette, blackjack and other card games, and dice games such as craps. Casinos use chips rather than money: small coloured disks of different monetary values which a gambler can purchase on their way in and exchange for cash again on leaving.

Cybergambling
Also called interactive, remote or online gambling. This refers to the rising trend of gambling remotely, using an Internet-enabled computer, interactive television or mobile phone. £5bn a year is currently wagered online, and estimates suggest that gambling by mobile phone will grow into a multi-million-pound business by 2009.

Fruit machines
Also called slot machines and one-armed bandits. These machines are coin-operated, and usually work by generating symbols on a dial, with different combinations winning different amounts of money for the player.

Gambling
An activity in which one or more persons place a stake (usually money) on an event whose outcome is uncertain ('placing a bet'). This can include horse or dog racing, card games, lotteries, casino games, betting machines and bingo.

Lottery
A chance numbers game where the customer has to select the winning numbers drawn out. The jackpot is a percentage of the money collected from everyone playing. Lotteries are often used to collect money for charity. In the UK, the most popular lottery is the National Lottery.

Problem gambling
Also called gambling addiction, pathological or compulsive gambling. A problem gambler is one who becomes addicted to the thrill of gambling in a similar way to a drug or alcohol addict; so much so that they no longer have any control over their gambling and will risk money, careers and relationships. The Salvation Army claims there are 370,000 problem gamblers in this country, although some worry that this number will rise with the advent of the new supercasino and growth in online gambling.

Scratchcard
A form of gambling in which the player purchases a card and scratches off the surface, revealing symbols hidden underneath. Certain combinations of symbols will result in a prize. The National Lottery produces scratchcards which are the most commonly purchased in the UK.

Spread betting
A high-risk form of gambling popular with people wishing to bet on the stock exchange and sporting events. Winnings can be large but gamblers have less control over how much they may lose.

Supercasino
The UK's first supercasino is currently being planned under the government's Gambling Act 2005. It will be an all-day Las Vegas-style gambling palace, which will be allowed to include 1,250 slot machines with a jackpot of £1m. Sometimes referred to as mega-casino or regional-casino. There are also plans for eight large casinos, which will have the right to operate 150 machines with jackpots of £5,000.

INDEX

addiction *see* problem gambling
addictiveness of gambling 30

benefits of gambling 18
betting 2
bingo 2
biological effects, compulsive gambling 29

casinos 2
  new, UK 15, 34
  supercasinos 14-16, 34
children and gambling
  online gambling 18
  protection by Gambling Commission 4
  Scotland 32-3
  see also underage gambling
compulsive gambling *see* problem gambling
Culture, Media and Sport, Department for (DCMS) and
  the Gambling Commission 5
cybergambling 17-26

Department for Culture, Media and Sport (DCMS) and
  the Gambling Commission 5
doctors, fears of gambling rise 31
drug treatment for gambling 39

effects of gambling 36
  physical 29, 36
  psychological 6, 29
  research 16
employees, gambling 22-4
Europe, online gambling 20

fruit machines 2
  and under 16s 11

GamAnon 37
gamblers, help for *see* help for problem gamblers
Gamblers Anonymous 37
gambling
  addiction *see* problem gambling
  addictiveness 30
  benefits 18
  controlled 2, 28
  definition 1, 28
  effects *see* effects of gambling
  forms of 2
  history 1
  by mobiles 18, 26
  and neurobiology 6
  problems *see* problem gambling
  signs *see* signs of problem gambling
  social factors 7, 29
  statistics 1-3, 4
  at work 22-4
Gambling Act 5, 17, 23

Gambling Commission, The 4-5
  licence conditions 8, 23
gambling psychology 6
Gaming Board for Great Britain 4
good causes, money raised by gambling 18
  National Lottery 9

help for problems gamblers 5, 29, 36
  drug treatment 39
  support groups 37
history of gambling 1

impulse control disorder drug, treatment for gambling 39
interactive gambling 17-26
Internet gambling *see* online gambling
Internet National Lottery games, and under 16s 12-13

law
  Gambling Act 5, 17, 23
  and gambling at work 23
  and online gambling 17
licensing and the Gambling Commission 5, 8, 23
lotteries 2
  see also National Lottery

market size, gambling industry 4
  National Lottery 9, 10
  online gambling 17, 19
mobile gambling 18, 26

nalmefene 39
National Lottery 9-10
  and under 16s 11-13
neurobiology and gambling 6

Olympic Games funding, National Lottery 9
online gambling 17-18, 19-25
  and addiction 21-2
  Europe 20
  National Lottery games, under 16s 12-13
  participation rates 17, 19
  poker, underage 25
  at work 22-4

Paralympic Games funding, National Lottery 9
participation in gambling 4
  National Lottery 9, 10
  online gambling 19
  young people 11
pathological gambling *see* problem gambling
poker, online, and underage gambling 25
problem gambling 2, 27-39
  causes 29
  definition 11
  drug treatment 39
  and Gambling Commission 5

help for 5, 29, 36, 37, 39
online gambling 21-2
signs 28, 29, 35-6, 38
support groups 37
under 16s 13, 25, 32-3
women 34
psychology and gambling 6, 29

remote gambling 17-26

Scotland, children and gambling 32-3
scratchcards and under 16s 12
sensible gambling 2, 28
signs of problem gambling 28, 29, 35-6, 38
at work 22-3, 24
social activity, gambling as 18
social factors and gambling 7, 29
social gambling 11
spending on gambling 4
children 32, 33
mobile gambling 26
National Lottery 9, 10
online gambling 17, 19
Scotland 32
United States 27
sports betting 2
spread betting 2
statistics 1-3, 4
super casinos 14-16, 34
support for gamblers *see* help for problem gamblers

tax revenues from gambling 18

underage gambling 1
National Lottery 11-13
online gambling 18, 25
online poker 25
Scotland 32-3
United Kingdom
online gambling market 19, 20
super casino 14-16
United States
participation in gambling 27
and underage online poker 25

winning
chances of 36
National Lottery 9
withdrawal symptoms 30
women
gambling addiction 21, 34
online gambling addiction 27
work, gambling at 22-4

young people and gambling 1
gambling addiction 25, 31, 32-3
National Lottery 11-13
signs of gambling problems 38
views on gambling 13

Additional Resources

Other Issues titles

If you are interested in researching further some of the issues raised in *Gambling Trends*, you may like to read the following titles in the **Issues** series:

⇨ Vol. 118 *Focus on Sport* (ISBN 978 1 86168 351 9)

⇨ Vol. 110 *Poverty* (ISBN 978 1 86168 343 4)

⇨ Vol. 107 *Work Issues* (ISBN 978 1 86168 327 4)

⇨ Vol. 104 *Our Internet Society* (ISBN 978 1 86168 324 3)

⇨ Vol. 84 *Mental Wellbeing* (ISBN 978 1 86168 279 6)

⇨ Vol. 83 *Dealing with Crime* (ISBN 978 1 86168 278 9)

⇨ Vol. 74 *Money Matters* (ISBN 978 1 86168 263 5)

⇨ Vol. 43 *A Consumer Society* (ISBN 978 1 86168 204 8)

For more information about these titles, visit our website at www.independence.co.uk/publicationslist

Useful organisations

You may find the websites of the following organisations useful for further research:

⇨ Camelot: www.camelotgroup.co.uk

⇨ Carole Spiers Group: www.carolespiersgroup.com

⇨ Economic and Social Research Council: www.esrc.ac.uk

⇨ FirstScience: www.firstscience.com

⇨ Gamblers Anonymous: www.gamblersanonymous.org.uk

⇨ Gambling Commission: www.gamblingcommission.gov.uk

⇨ GamCare: www.gamcare.org.uk

⇨ Mental Health Foundation: www.mentalhealth.org.uk

⇨ National Lottery Commission: www.natlotcomm.gov.uk

⇨ Nielsen//NetRatings: www.nielsen-netratings.com

⇨ Salvation Army: www.salvationarmy.org.uk

⇨ TheSite: www.thesite.org

⇨ Virgin.net: www.virgin.net

ACKNOWLEDGEMENTS

The publisher is grateful for permission to reproduce the following material.

While every care has been taken to trace and acknowledge copyright, the publisher tenders its apology for any accidental infringement or where copyright has proved untraceable. The publisher would be pleased to come to a suitable arrangement in any such case with the rightful owner.

Chapter One: Gambling in the UK

Gambling, © GamCare, Forms of gambling, © GamCare, The Gambling Commission, © Gambling Commission, The science of gambling, © FirstScience. com, Governing gambling, © Gambling Commission, Key facts about the National Lottery, © Camelot, Lottery timeline, © National Lottery Commission, Under 16s and the National Lottery, © Ipsos MORI/ National Lottery Commission, UK's first supercasino, © virgin.net, Q&A: Supercasino, © Guardian Newspapers Ltd 2006, Risks of the 'supercasino', © Economic and Social Research Council, Interactive or remote gambling, © Ethical Investment Advisory Group of the Church of England, Are there any benefits to gambling?, © Ethical Investment Advisory Group of the Church of England.

Chapter Two: Cybergambling

Boom in online gambling, © 999Today, Online gambling in Europe, © Nielsen//NetRatings, Online gambling drives addiction rates, © vnunet.com, Internet betting, © Telegraph Group Ltd 2006, Gambling at work, © Carole Spiers, £1m online loser jailed, © Telegraph Group Ltd 2006, Online poker hooks teenagers, © Guardian Newspapers Ltd 2006, Mobile gambling boom time ahead, © 2006 CNET Networks Inc.

Chapter Three: Problem Gambling

The problem with gambling, © virgin.net, Information on gambling, © Mental Health Foundation, Gambling 'as addictive as crack cocaine', © 2006 Associated Newspapers Ltd, Doctors fear boom in gambling addiction, © Press Association, One in 10 Scottish children is gambling addict, © Scotsman Publications Ltd, Story of a teenage problem gambler, © Salvation Army, More women seeking help over gambling addiction, © Press Association, Signs and interventions for a gambling dependency, © GamCare, Gambling debt, © TheSite.org, Gamblers Anonymous and GamAnon, © Gamblers Anonymous, Drug may curb pathological gambling, © American Psychiatric Association.

Photographs and illustrations:

Pages 1, 24, 31, 39: Simon Kneebone; pages 5, 14, 27, 34: Don Hatcher; pages 6, 22, 30, 35: Angelo Madrid; pages 26, 28: Bev Aisbett.

And with thanks to the team: Mary Chapman, Sandra Dennis and Jan Haskell.

Lisa Firth
Cambridge
January, 2007